THE

Man That Rum Made

WITH

Temperance Lessons and Stories

"Every man that striveth for the mastery is temperate in all things." "So run, that ye may obtain."

CHARCTER CLASSICS
VOLUME THREE

Edited by
J. E. WHITE AND MRS. **L. D. AVERY-STUTTLE**

PUBLISHED BY
SOUTHERN PUBLISHING ASSOCIATION
NASHVILLE, TENN.

CONTENTS

DANGER SIGNALS

hIS is the man
that rum made

DANGER-
SIGNALS

THIS is the weed
that sowed the seed
For making the man,
that rum made

DANGER:
SIGNALS

ᚻIS is the cider,
the rumseller's tinder,
That goes with the weed
that sowed the seed
For making the man
that rum made

DANGER SIGNALS

HIS is the beer,
  the jolly good lager,
Firm friend of cider,
  the rumseller's tinder,
That goes with the weed
  that sowed the seed
For making the man
  that rum made

DANGER
SIGNALS

HIS is the wine,
the red, red wine,
Alluring from beer,
the jolly good lager,
Firm friend of cider,
the rumseller's tinder,
That goes with the weed
that sowed the seed
For making the man,
that rum made

DANGER-
SIGNALS

HIS is the whisky,
to make you tipsy,
That follows the wine,
the red, red wine,,
Alluring from beer,
the jolly good lager,
Firm friend of cider,
the rumseller's tinder,
That goes with the weed
that sowed the seed
For making the man,
that rum made

HIS is the nose that blossoms and grows
On the face of the man that
   rum made.

HIS is the cheek, all flabby and weak,
By the side of the nose that blossoms and grows
On the face of the man that rum made.

 HIS is the eye, all bleared and awry,

Surmounting the cheek, so flabby and weak,

By the side of the nose that blossoms and grows

On the face of the man that rum made.

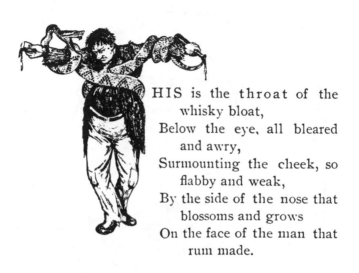

HIS is the throat of the
    whisky bloat,
Below the eye, all bleared
    and awry,
Surmounting the cheek, so
    flabby and weak,
By the side of the nose that
    blossoms and grows
On the face of the man that
    rum made.

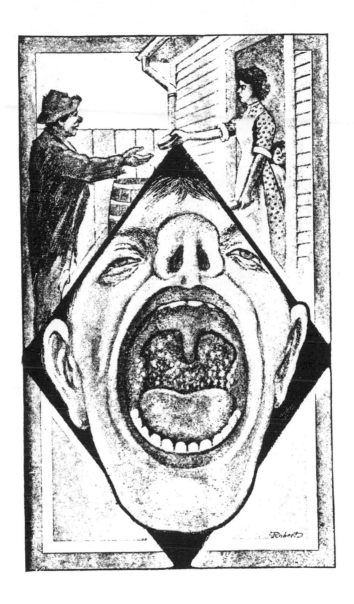

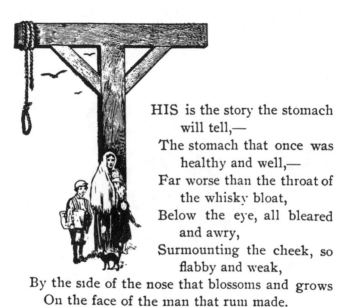

HIS is the story the stomach
    will tell,—
The stomach that once was
    healthy and well,—
Far worse than the throat of
    the whisky bloat,
Below the eye, all bleared
    and awry,
Surmounting the cheek, so
    flabby and weak,
By the side of the nose that blossoms and grows
On the face of the man that rum made.

A Healthy Stomach B Stomach of Drunkard
C Stomach of Drunkard with Delirium Tremens

HIS is the liver, all pickled and
    shrunk,
Produced by the alcohol, making
    him drunk,
Thus aiding the story the stom-
    ach will tell,—
The stomach that once was heal-
    thy and well,—
Far worse than the throat of the whisky bloat,
Below the eye, all bleared and awry,
Surmounting the cheek, so flabby and weak,
By the side of the nose that blossoms and grows
On the face of the man that rum made.

HIS is the group of little blood cells,
Each crippled and killed by the poison which tells,
So fatal to liver, all pickled and shrunk,
Produced by the alcohol, making him drunk,
Thus aiding the story the stomach will tell,—
The stomach that once was healthy and well,—
Far worse than the throat of the whisky bloat,
Below the eye, all bleared and awry,
Surmounting the cheek, so flabby and weak,
By the side of the nose that blossoms and grows
On the face of the man that rum made.

HIS is the wreck that alcohol
        made
Of the man who once was
        sober and staid,
Whose blood was diseased
        by the little blood cells
Being crippled or killed by
        the poison which tells,
So fatal to liver, all pickled
        and shrunk,
Produced by the alcohol, making him drunk,
Thus aiding the story the stomach will tell,—
The stomach that once was healthy and well,—
Far worse than the throat of the whisky bloat,
Below the eye, all bleared and awry,
Surmounting the cheek, so flabby and weak,
By the side of the nose that blossoms and grows
        On the face of the man that rum made.

Grandma Duncan and the Children

OLD JOE, THE DRUNKARD

By Mrs. L. D. Avery-Stuttle

 GRANDMA DUNCAN lived with her three grandchildren in a pleasant village nestled among the green hills of New Hampshire. Grandmother had a habit of taking the children, Bertha, Max, and Henri, out for a walk over the hills, on pleasant days, and much the children enjoyed these rambles.

"There is nothing," grandmother used to say, "that I so desire as to see the children of my dear daughter (who left them to my care,) grow up to be good and virtuous."

Grandmother's hair was white as snow, but her eyes were as bright and blue as the skies, her voice was soft and tender, and the children of the whole neighborhood loved to listen to her quaint stories of the time when she was a child; while to Bertha, Max, and Henri, grandmother was very dear.

One afternoon, when the May flowers were showing their pretty, fresh faces on the hills and meadows, and the sun was shining brightly, they all went for their accustomed walk. The children soon filled their baskets with trailing arbutus, jon-

3

quils, and soft mosses, and just as the sun was setting, grandma and little Bertha strolled leisurely homeward, while Max and Henri hurried on before.

"You shall be Queen of the May, grandma, dear," laughed Bertha. "See, I shall crown you with these pretty jonquils as soon as we are home."

Just then Max and Henri came running back panting and quite out of breath, both eager to tell what they had just seen over the hill.

"O grandma!" began Henri, "there is a poor man lying asleep by the bridge, all covered with mud—"

"Yes," added Max, "yes, and his face is red and specked, and—O Henri, did you notice that his old battered hat was floating

POOR OLD JOE

around in that pool of muddy water by his side?"

"I'm afraid it is poor Joe Brandon," sighed grandma. "Let us hasten; perhaps we may be able to help him. He may be really ill,—though much I fear he has stayed too long at the Red Lion," as the one saloon in the village was named.

By this time poor Joe had awakened from his drunken stupor, and was staggering on toward his wretched home as fast as his unsteady legs would carry him. His filth-covered coat was reeking with slime and mud, which constantly dripped over his ragged trousers, while his wet and battered hat, which the poor fellow had contrived to rescue from the pool, was slouched far over his face. His gray hair and beard were long and matted, and his eyes were bleared and bloodshot.

The children shrank as far away from him as possible, as he reeled past them, and all the laughter and pleasant mirth had gone out of their voices, while little Bertha's face had grown quite white.

"I cannot blame you, my dears, for shunning the wretched man, and yet he was not always so," sighed grandma.

"Why grandma," protested Henri, who thought himself quite a man, "he has been a poor drunkard ever since I can remember,—and that is ever and ever so many years,—why just think; I am almost twelve years old."

"Yes, but you know, my dear, I can remember very many more years than that,—and I knew poor old Joe when he was no more than five years old.   And a sweet, charming child he used to be."

"O grandma! please tell us about it," cried the children excitedly, "please do!"

So as soon as they were home and well rested, they gathered around grandma's great rocking chair.   Henri had kindled a fire in the grate, for it was rather cool, and now they waited to hear the story she had promised to tell them.

"Well, my children," she began, "it is quite true that I knew poor old Joe when he was a sweet, innocent child,—I was a child myself, then,"—and grandmother gazed dreamily at the red flames as they chased each other up the chimney.

"Yes, he was a sweet, inno-cent child," she repeated; "Nobody called him 'Old Joe,' then.   He was the only son of my father's dear friend, and I was his playmate while we were children."

"O grandmother!" said lit-tle Bertha.   "How could he ever grow to be such a bad man?"

"It was not all at once, my child, but little by little. You remember the tiny seed you planted in

LITTLE JOB

the pot last year and how we watched it day by day as it grew slowly. Don't you remember how it put out first one little green leaf after another until it became a tall, strong plant?"

"Yes, grandma, it was so small I thought it would not grow at first, but I watered it and kept it in the sunny window, and now it's quite a big tree."

"Well, my child, it is just so with bad habits. They grow just as fast as weeds.

"I will try to tell you all about it, my children, though it is a long story. I hope you will listen thoughtfully, for poor old Joe's life story is almost the same as that of many thousands of poor drunkards in this rum-cursed land."

"O grandma! are there thousands of people as miserable and wretched as this poor man?" questioned Henri, opening his brown eyes wide; "'t doesn't seem at all possible. I'm so sorry for them," he continued, for Henri had a very tender heart and was full of sympathy for every one in trouble.

"I hope you will be sorry for them," replied grandma, "so sorry that you will do all in your power, as long as you live, to help them to lead better lives and to shun the very first step toward a life of intemperance and shame; for you must not forget, my boy, that no man becomes a worthless sot in a day or a month or even a year. In this, as in everything else, the little things are those which count. Indeed, life is made up of little things,—

little duties neglected, little deeds undone, little burdens unborne,—these all help to make a careless, selfish, unlovely character.

"I remember that poor Joe was very selfish as a lad, and this most undesirable trait grew upon him as the years went by, until finally he would not scruple to do anything mean, or rude, or anything dishonest, if thereby he might gratify his appetite."

"What do you think the poor old man would have said," questioned Max, "when he was a young boy, to have seen a picture of himself as he looked to-day, wallowing in the mud, just like the big pig in Mr. Brown's meadow!" and Max shuddered.

"He would have been greatly shocked, I dare say, but I almost question whether, then, he would have been willing to quit his selfish and gluttonous habits ; for poor Joe was a great glutton, even when a small boy," explained grandma, "though, as I have said, he was a bright and lovable little fellow."

"A great glutton !" repeated Max wonderingly. "I supposed a glutton was a person who ate too much food. I didn't think that the kind or amount of food a person ate had anything to do with his becoming a drunkard. Does it grandma?" And Max awaited the reply of his grandma with some anxiety, for he was very fond of sweets and rich pastry.

"Yes, yes, my child ; the kind and quantity of food we eat has very much to do with the making or spoiling of our lives."

"Joe's father and mother were good people, who

tried to bring their little boy up to control his appetite; for they were wise and prudent, and well knew the evil effects of gluttony upon both body and soul. But they died when Joe was very young, and left him to the care of his aunt.

"Aunt Maggie was a good woman, but she made a great mistake in allowing Joe to eat anything and everything he wanted, and at any time he pleased. She seemed to forget that the stomach needs rest as well as the other parts of the body, when we are tired."

"Isn't that queer?" laughed Bertha. "I never thought of it in that way before."

"Many people either forget or do not know that this is true," continued grandma, "and overload their poor, tired stomachs, and force them to work when they are weary and need rest, until they become weak and wretched and full of disease.

"Joe was very fond of sweetmeats," continued grandma, looking hard at Max, "but at first, he contented himself with coaxing his aunt for them. But when he grew larger, he did not always wait to ask for candies and preserves and rich cake. Aunt Maggie, as we called her, kept a large supply of rich and highly seasoned food constantly on hand, and when Joe was ashamed to ask for any more, he would manage to steal as much as he wanted from the cupboard. This he did quite often, and it troubled me not a little," and grandma sighed.

"Why didn't you tell your mother or Aunt

Maggie of the young rascal?" interrupted Henri, who scorned anything like falsehood or theft.

"I feared that he would not play with me if I did; but I have regretted my childish thoughtlessness many times; for perhaps if I had been more faithful in doing what I could for him, poor Joe might not now be the miserable wreck he is."

"Just think of our grandmother ever wanting to play with that horrible old creature!" exclaimed Bertha, "though of course he was not always so; but I can't see, yet, grandma, what all this has to do with making poor Joe a drunkard. Will you tell us?"

"If you will be patient, my child. It is quite a long story, and I want you to be fully impressed with its truthfulness, and to understand me.

"One day I went over to play with Joey, as we children used to call him. I was only about five years old, and Joey was six. My parents thought him a good child, and since he was the son of my father's best-loved friend, they allowed me to play with him very often.

"Aunt Maggie had a jar of choice preserves, and another jar of highly seasoned and spiced pickles. These she kept in the cupboard on a high shelf, out of reach of naughty, mischievous fingers. That day after we had become tired of our blocks and marbles, Joey asked Aunt Maggie for a dish of preserves. She very kindly gave us each a dish, with some bread and butter, and shortly afterward, put on her bonnet to go down the street. She did not forget to caution us not to get into any mischief.

"But as soon as she was out of sight, Master Joey decided to have as many cookies and plates of preserves as he wanted. At once he climbed into a high chair and helped himself. I was never allowed such freedom as this at home, and in my childish way, tried to explain to my playfellow that it was wrong. But he paid small heed to my words and ate until he became quite sick.

"By this time Aunt Maggie had returned, and though poor Joey tried hard to deceive her as to the cause of his illness, the greedy boy had quite forgotten to wash his face, which, in his haste, had become smeared with preserves.

"Aunt Maggie made him drink a cupful of bitter herbs, and I ran home to my mother."

OLD JOE, THE DRUNKARD

PART TWO

NEXT day I went to see poor Joe, but he was too sick to play with me."

"I think he must have learned a lesson by this time, ventured Bertha."

"O no, my child, you see he has not even yet learned to control his appetite, and it has nearly proved his ruin, and surely must unless he repents very soon, and turns from his evil ways. Instead of learning a useful lesson from that day's folly, his craving for sweets and rich foods seemed to grow stronger from that time. He always called for the most highly seasoned food whenever he would come to spend the day with me,—the greasiest meat, the strongest pickles, the richest puddings.

"One day at our table my mother helped him to some food. At once Joey called for the pepper. 'It is not good for you, child,' said my mother, mildly. But Joey insisted until she allowed him to cover his food with pepper till it was quite black. He was very indignant indeed when mother told him that she never allowed me such highly seasoned food, and the young gentleman declared at once that if he could not have what he wanted to eat, he would go home where he could get as much as he pleased, and that he would never come to play with me again.

"O my children! I hope you will never forget that appetite is like fire;" and grandma sighed; "it is a good servant, but a bad master. You see that in poor Joe's case it has proved to be a strong giant, from whose dreadful chains he has no power to release himself."

"I suppose," ventured Bertha, "that he began drinking rum when he was just a little boy."

"PEPPER"

"O no; the taste for liquor is not formed in a moment. All this time he was an intelligent, bright, and active lad, and I liked to play with him very much. Until he was about eight years old, he drank nothing but water or milk. But by this time, the rich foods and spices, the pepper and the strong, fiery pickles, with which he had so often filled his stomach, created a longing for something stronger than milk and water to drink.

"'Come, Aunt Maggie,' he pleaded, one day, 'come; please let me have a little taste of your tea—just a little.'"

"Of course, he got it," said Bertha.

"O yes, and before long, he ran slily into the pantry, and drank still another large cup. When I threatened to tell Aunt Maggie, he only smiled and

"I love it, I tell you; it's good!"

replied: 'I love it, I tell you; it's good! if it doesn't hurt Aunt Maggie, it won't hurt me. If it's good for women, it's good for boys, and I shall have what I like—there now!'

"I was a timid little girl," continued grandma, smiling gravely, "and Joe's logic as well as his bravado rather appealed to me, and so I said nothing. When it came time for me to go home that day, he went a little piece with me, as was his custom:—

"'I wonder if Aunt Maggie thinks that was my first cup of tea,' reflected Joe, turning confidentially to me, ''cause if she does, she's mistaken, that's all;

and what's more, I've got so I just hanker after it—and good, strong coffee, too. Aunt Maggie thinks it's expensive, I guess; but I don't believe she thinks it hurts anybody, or she would not drink it herself. I tell you, Jennie Brown'—Joey used to call me by my full name whenever he was excited,—'when I get to be a man,—a big man, —I'll have what I want to eat,—I tell you,—and —and—*what I want to drink*, too, or I'll know the reason why!' he added, pompously bringing one little fist down into the palm of the other hand.

"'O Joey, Joey!' I cried; 'you don't mean to be a horrid old drunkard!' Joe flashed a look of defiance back at me:—

"'Don't you suppose, Jennie Brown, that I mean to be a gentleman—a gentleman, like my father used to be?—Well, I do, but I guess a little tea and coffee'll not hurt me any,—and look here, sissy, I'll tell you something if you'll never tell,' he continued, putting his small fingers across my lips; 'look here; I've noticed that a great many *gentlemen* smoke and chew tobacco, and just a soon as I get a little bigger,—you just wait!' and Joey assumed a swaggering gait, and puckering his red lips, puffed a cloud of imaginary smoke from an imaginary pipe. Then he turned on his heel, and called a cheery good-by to me.

"But into my young heart had crept a vague fear that between my little playmate and myself there would be, some day, '*a great gulf fixed*!'"

OLD JOE, THE DRUNKARD

PART THREE

I T doesn't seem a bit possible!" exclaimed Bertha, "that this awful looking old man could have been a nice little boy,—nice enough to *ever* have been my grandma's playmate!"

"No," reflected Max, "I didn't dream that just tea and coffee ever helped to make drunkards,—very many people surely use them both, —nice people, too, grandma."

"But it does not always have this effect, my dear, and we may be thankful, but it is certainly one of the stepping stones to intemperance."

"But I don't understand why," said Max, who always wanted to know the reason for everything. "Can't you tell us, grandma, why tea and coffee are so bad? 'Cause if they are, I'll never drink another cup of either again, as long as I live,—for I don't want to run any risk at all of being a drunkard,—isn't that what you say, too, Henri?"

"Indeed, it is,—no drunkard for me, I tell you! but may be grandma will tell us a little more about it," and Henri put his boyish cheek close to grandma's and gave her two or three hearty kisses. "Please tell us, grandma."

"Well, my children, both tea and coffee contain

(46)

a very deadly poison, but in so small a quantity that we do not at once feel the evil effects."

"No, grandma; I have often heard Mrs. Wilson, the grocer's wife, say that she could not work until she had had her cup of tea."

"That is because it stimulates the system," said grandma. "I will make

Mrs. Wilson's Tea   The Whip

it plain to you. Do you remember in our walk this afternoon, we saw a cruel driver whipping his poor horse to make him pull his heavy load up the hill?"

"Yes, yes; and I felt like snatching the whip away from the wicked man," said Henri.

"It would have been wiser and better for him to take off a part of the load instead of whipping his poor, patient horse. Still, you remember how much quicker the poor beast drew his burden to the top.

"Now, my children, tea and coffee act on the body just as the driver's whip did upon the horse. Perhaps we can do more work at the time by drinking it, but, like the horse, when we have done the work, we are completely exhausted, and feel the need of more and more of the poison."

"I just knew grandma could make it plain to you boys," smiled Bertha,—"but I believe *I* understood it quite well all the time. But please go on with the story about Joe, grandma, I want to see how it all comes out."

"Why, my child, you *saw* how it came out,—saw it all too plainly, this afternoon, when you saw poor old Joe as he reeled by us," and grandma sighed, while a tear stole down her cheeks. "Yes, you *saw* how my story must end; but I will tell you the steps which poor Joe next took:—

"When he was about ten years old, I went over again one day to play with him. As I have said, he was a pleasant and lively playfellow, generally good natured, and always ready to build me playhouses and never laughed at my dolls.

"After we had played for some time, Joey began to act uneasy. 'What's the matter, Joey?' I asked. 'See, you are spoiling my playhouse, and it just suited me. You act as if you didn't want to play at all; I'll go right home unless,—"

"'O, don't be a silly sissy!' exclaimed Joey, 'I didn't mean to spoil your playhouse,—but, look here, Jennie Brown, *I'm* getting dreadful thirsty!'

"'Well, then, go and get a drink of water. See,

Aunt Maggie has just pumped a nice fresh pail.

"'See here' said Joey, 'you need n't think I'm such a sissy and ninny as to drink *water* when I can get something else that's a whole lot better!'

"He winked at me very slily, and turning on his

heel, he beckoned me to follow. I was so curious to know what he was going to do, that I dropped my

"You oughtn't to do that, Joey."

dolls and scampered after him. As we passed the kitchen window, he peeped in cautiously, to assure himself that Aunt Maggie was so busy that she would not be apt to see him, and then he again beckoned me to follow him down the back cellar stairs:—

"'What are you going to do, Joey?' I whispered, almost frightened at his strange actions.

"'Sh—sh—! speak lower. See! I'm going to have a good drink of Aunt Maggie's cider. She's been saving it for weeks and weeks to make vinegar of,—but it's good enough to suit me, now,' he chuckled, as he produced a long straw, and, inserting it in the hole of the barrel, took a long, deep draft, and offered the straw to me:—

4

"'I tell you, it's good. Come, help yourself. It makes a fellow feel nice all over. When I take a little bit too much, it gives me a headache, and Aunt Maggie makes me a good, strong cup of tea,' he chuckled, 'so I don't care very much after all.'"

"But did you drink, grandma?" gasped Bertha.

"I tasted it, but it was so bitter I couldn't drink it, nor did I want to do so. Then we tip-toed back into the kitchen. Aunt Maggie gave Joe a keen glance, but she said nothing, and we hurried out again to our play.

"'You ought n't to do that, Joey,' I said, looking fearlessly into his bright brown eyes, 'I just know you ought not; what would Aunt Maggie say?'

"'It doesn't harm her any,' he returned; 'the old lady will have a little less vinegar, that's all,—I prefer my vinegar *this* way. I've had all I've wanted to drink for a month, and it gets better and better,—and, besides, I can drink a whole lot more than I could at first, and it's lots stronger, too. After a little I guess I can drink as much as a big man and never feel it!' and poor Joey stretched himself to his greatest height, and strutted about the playhouse in an exceedingly silly manner."

"Why didn't you tell Aunt Maggie?" asked Bertha. "I would have told my mother, at least."

"Perhaps you would, but I was a thoughtless child, and Joey was almost the only playmate I had, and as I was very fond of play, I suppose I kept quiet from a selfish fear that I might be forbidden his company entirely."

OLD JOE, THE DRUNKARD

PART FOUR

IT doesn't seem possible,—I declare it doesn't!" exclaimed Henri, "that anybody could ever have cared to be near that horrid old man,—least of all, our nice, sweet grandma."

"But you must not forget that he was not *always horrid.* He was as fair and bright then, as you are, Max. And I tell you, my children, if you are ever led to follow in his steps, and form the appetite for strong drink which he did, you would not be one whit better in appearance or condition in a few years than old Joe is to-day. It may well make you shudder, my boy, but I tell you the truth, and I only hope you will keep the object lesson which you have learned to-day always before you.

"I did not dream, at this time, any more than poor Joe, what this would lead to.

"A few days after this," continued grandma, "his aunt sent him to our house to do an errand for her, and told him he might stay half an hour. After a little, while we were quietly playing, I noticed that Joey began acting strangely. When he tried to talk, his tongue seemed thick, and his eyes were red and dull.

"'What's the matter, Joey?' I asked, in real alarm, for I had never seen any one act so before.

"'Nothin' smatter. Little too much Aunt Magsh shider. Bezzer go home now,' and poor Joe walked unsteadily down the lane to the road. But even

"Bezzer go home now"

then it did not occur to me that my little playmate was actually a trifle drunk. I only thought he was trying to plague me, or was possibly a little sick, so I didn't mention it. But the very next week I was sent to Aunt Maggie's to borrow a pattern. When I asked for Joey, she said she guessed he was around somewhere, she didn't know where, she hadn't seen him all the morning.

"Of course, I scampered off to find him, for I wanted to spend the precious hour that mother had allotted me in which to play with Joey, in repairing our latest playhouse.

"'Joey! Joey!' I called. 'Come quick! For I can't stay very long. Come and let's mend the playhouse!'

"But there was no answer. I called again and again. It took me a long time to find him, but at last, just as I was getting a little frightened, I turned around a corner of the old barn, and there, leaning against the corncrib, with his round face

quite white, was Master Joey, sucking away bravely
on an old clay pipe which we had often used to
blow soap bubbles with.

"The smell of the tobacco smoke was quite
strong, so I knew at once what my poor young
friend was attempting to do. I had heard my
father say that smoking was a very bad habit, and

"His round face quite white"

the smell of the nasty suff made
me feel sick, myself, for I was
not accustomed to it.

"When Joe saw that he was
fairly caught, he tried to put on
an air of great importance, and began stuffing
more of the vile tobacco into his pipe; but I could
see that his hand trembled so that he could hardly
hold the pipe.

"'Why, Joe Brandon!' I exclaimed, now fairly
aroused. 'I'll tell Aunt Maggie, there now,—I
declare, I will!' and I started toward the house.

"'Come back, I tell you! I wouldn't be a little telltale!' shouted Joey, though his voice sounded weak and strange. 'You just march back here, Miss Tattler, or I'll never build you another playhouse as long as I live, or play with you another minute. Every single time a fellow wants to have a little fun, then you begin to threaten to tell Aunt Maggie! As much as I've done for you,—and as many playhouses as I've made for you! Never you mind, Miss Tattler, it's the last—the very last!'

"My children, I am ashamed to say I hung my head and slowly sauntered back; but I felt guilty.

"Joe tried to laugh boisterously, as he saw me coming back, and though he was really a kind-hearted boy, he began to mock me, and threatened to tell my mother that I had stolen the tobacco from the grocery for him.

"'But you know that isn't true, Joe Brandon!' I protested with trembling voice, for it was the first quarrel we had ever had.

"'I'm no sissy boy, I'll have you understand, Miss Jennie Brown! Lots of the best and richest men in town smoke. Even the new minister smokes cigars, for I saw him, and I'm going to smoke, too. It's no worse for me than it is for them. So there! I guess you'll hold your tongue now, Miss Jennie Brown!'"

"Why, grandma!" exclaimed Henri; "he was surely very impolite, for a boy who was trying so hard to be a man. He deserved a good flogging;

if I'd been there, I never would have allowed him to speak like that to my grandma."

"Surely Joe must have been a bad boy. Did he ever talk to you like that before?" asked Bertha, whose face had grown very red.

"O no, Bertha; but you see one cannot expect much from a glutton or an intemperate person. And poor Joe had been a glutton so long and had taxed his weak stomach so many years with rich food, and stimulating tea and coffee, pepper and spices, that all this began to be felt in his nervous system, and led to all sorts of evil; until, when he was only ten years old, he had such a craving for something strong and exciting that he began learning the tabacco habit. The Bible says truly that none can bring a clean thing out of an unclean. So, how could sweet and gentle words come from lips through which passed so much calculated to destroy and break down the body and ruin the nervous system?"

"Did Aunt Maggie find it out at last?" questioned Max.

"O yes; I will tell you about it; finally after Joe had smoked his pipe out, I said to him, 'come, now; my hour is almost up, and I've been waiting for you all this time. I hope you are ready to come with me now and fix our new playhouse.' Then I turned to look at Joe. I tell you, children, I *was* frightened this time and no mistake. The poor lad's eyes were turned up and rolling wildly in their sockets. His cheeks were as white as marble and his lips were purple and drawn; his hands were clenched, and he rolled down like a log by the side of the straw stack. Still he groaned, 'don't you tell Aunt Maggie—no, no!'

"'I must! I must! I guess

"He'll die, won't he?"

you are going to die, Joey, I must call her! I can't let you die here, all alone!'
But all poor Joe could do was just to curl up in a heap, and snarl, 'Tattle, tattle!' between groans.

"I was just deciding to run home and leave him to his fate, for surely I thought him dying, when I looked up, and there stood Aunt Maggie. She took in the situation at a glance. She had begun to worry about Joe's being gone so long, and had started out to find us.

"There, by the side of the sick and spueing lad, lay the old pipe, the cause of all the mischief. The good lady was terribly disgusted, besides being considerably frightened. For a moment she did not speak, though her lips trembled ; I was the first to scream :—

"'O Aunt Maggie! he'll die, won't he?'

"'Die?—No; but may be it would be better in the end if he should, before he breaks all our hearts.'

"Aunt Maggie was large and strong, and I had always thought her too stouthearted to cry, but something very much like a sob broke from her trembling lips, as she said, not unkindly, kneeling by the side of the sick boy, and putting his damp head in her motherly arms :—

"'Joe, lad, I've been *thinking* all wasn't right with you of late. I've been missing the hard cider in the cellar, and I've thought you acted strange. No wonder. Now, Joe, if this doesn't kill you, you must stop it at once. Where did you get the stuff?'

"'I'll not tell you! I'll die first!' groaned Joe.

"That's all I heard," continued grandma, "for I turned on my heel, and ran just as fast as my little feet could fly, nor stopped until I reached home, a very frightened and a very breathless little girl."

OLD JOE, THE DRUNKARD

PART FIVE

UT Aunt Maggie insisted upon knowing where Joe got the tobacco," said grandma, "and how he obtained the the money for buying it; for she found some of the nasty stuff hidden away in his room that same day. So, at supper, she again asked him to tell her the truth, and begged him to hide nothing from her. Aunt Maggie told my mother all about it afterward. She said that Joey had been doing errands for the grocer, Mr. Green, for some time, and that he had never brought home any money, and that now Joey declared that he had taken his pay in tobacco, because Mr. Green refused to pay him in any other way."

"That wasn't true, I dare say," reflected Max. "Was it, grandmother?"

"No, indeed. When Mr. Green found out about it, he said that he had paid the boy the money for all that he had done, and that he had not only not given him any tobacco, but that he did not keep it for sale at all in his shop. He said that as he knew

it to be harmful, he had decided not to sell the
stuff. So poor Aunt Maggie saw at once that Joey
had added to his other sins, those of falsehood and
deceit."

"Why, grandma," ventured Bertha, "I should
think you would not have wanted to play with him
any more, when you saw what a bad, deceitful boy
he was."

"No, I did not play with him any more. My
father at once forebade that, and in a few weeks
Aunt Maggie moved away. Of course, I missed
my old playfellow, but I did not see him again in a
long time," continued grandma. "My mother saw
Aunt Maggie after they had been gone about a
year, and mother said that she never saw such a sad
change in any one before. The poor old lady's hair
had grown quite white, and her face was pale and
careworn."

"I dare say that bad, ungrateful boy vexed her
so that she had no peace," continued Bertha.

"Yes, yes," sighed grandma, "my mother said
there were tears in Aunt Maggie's eyes as she told
her that poor Joe was going to ruin as fast as he
could, and that already she found it quite impossible to control him.

"Finally, one day about three or four years after
this, my father had occasion to pass through the
town where Joey lived, and I went with him. I
rather hoped we would not see Joe, for I knew that
the meeting would be only painful; for you will
remember that by this time I had grown to be a large

girl,—quite a young lady, in fact, and Joe was a year older."

"Did Joe know you were coming?" asked Henri.

"O, no, or surely I do not think I should have found him in the place where he was."

"Maybe he wouldn't have cared after all," ventured Max.

"O, yes, he would, I am sure; for he was naturally a very proud lad, fond of show, and always anxious to make a good impression upon his friends. But you see, he didn't know we were coming, and so as father and I were passing the door of one of the many saloons which cursed the little town, there stood my old playfellow, among a crowd of young toughs, just in the act of lighting his pipe, and taking dreadful lessons in beer dinking and profanity. O you can't think how badly I felt."

"What did he say then, grandma? Wasn't he very much ashamed?" asked Bertha.

"Perhaps so. He stood close outside, by the door, and I called to him just as he was stepping inside. At first he pretended not to hear me, but it seemed to me that I could not let him enter that awful place; and so I ventured to call his name once more, louder than before. He could hardly refuse, then, to come back and speak to me. Just as he did so, an old man came out, staggering and spueing as he came. The man was quite well dressed, for this was one of the better saloons; but the poor man's face was red and bloated and looked much like old Joe's to-day.

"I could see that my young friend was considerably ashamed, but he tried by falsehood and deceit, and by putting on a bold front, to excuse the fact of his being in such a place.

"'Fact is, Mr. Brown,' he said, addressing my father, 'I was in there just doing an errand for Aunt Maggie. She wanted some alcohol for her camphor, and of course, *she* wouldn't go, so she coaxed me. I don't like these rough fellows, myself, Jennie,' he continued blandly. 'You know I never did. Didn't we have some jolly times in the old days though?' and I fancied," continued grandma, "that I could see a shade of real regret in his expressive brown eyes. O I felt so sorry for him!

"'Poor Joe!' I said, 'Aunt Maggie might a great deal better have gone without her camphor, than to send you into a saloon among those awful spueing men. Really, Joey,' I questioned in an undertone, 'did Aunt Maggie actually and truly send you?'

"'O you're just like you used to be, Jennie,' said he, laughing lightly, but I could see that my question made him wince. 'Of course she sent me, I have to mind Aunt Maggie, don't you see?'

"Finally, before I left him, I had made him promise solemnly that he would keep away from the saloons and never touch another glass of beer as long as he lived."

"Then he owned up, did he?" questioned Max.

"Yes, for he must have known on second thought, that his wretched falsehood about Aunt

Maggie's sending him into a saloon was too foolish to be believed."

"Well, anyway," sighed Bertha, "the poor boy didn't keep his promise to you, grandma, or we would not have seen him in the gutter to-day."

"O no, my dear; but it was all I could do, and perhaps it did affect him for good for a little while; for though he was weak and foolish and had, by this time, acquired a great love for the fatal cup, yet he had great respect for my father, and also entertained a strong feeling of freindship for me. Still, it took me some time to get him to make the promise.

"*I'll promise, of course.*"

"'You're asking a great deal of me, Jennie,' he said, 'seems to me you're pretty hard on a fellow, but I'll promise, of course. Though you ought to know me well enough to be perfectly assured that I would have too much sense to drink enough to do me any harm. Just a social glass now and again,—

that's all,—couldn't possibly do me a bit of harm. I flatter myself I'm too much of a gentleman not to know enough to quit when I've had plenty. Of course some people can't do it, but I am my father's son, Miss Jennie, and they say that he was a gentleman!' and the poor, misguided lad straightened himself very proudly and glanced at my father as though hoping he would approve his logic."

"What did your father say, grandma," queried Henri.

"He only smiled sadly at the self-conceited young lad and said:—

"'I used to know and love your father, Joe, he was a true gentleman, and one of my dearest friends,—indeed, he was too much of a gentleman to allow anything that could intoxicate to pass his lips. I only wish you would follow in his steps.'

"This sort of thing was not to Joe's liking one bit" continued grandma, "and he soon made an excuse to part company from us. He turned down another street, and it was nearly five years before I saw him again. Meanwhile, his heartbroken aunt, who had been to him both father and mother, was doing all in her power to save him.

"'I can't imagine whom the boy takes after,' she often said to my mother. 'None of his people ever drank, and his father was a gentleman.' But the poor woman did not realize that he had formed the love for strong drink right at home in her own pantry and cellar.

OLD JOE, THE DRUNKARD

PART SIX

AS I said, it was almost five years before I saw Joe Brandon again. He was then a young man of very fascinating manners, handsome, and attractive. But he was already becoming so idle and vicious that no one dared trust him, and although his face was handsome, his follies and intemperate habits had stamped themselves upon it, until they had given him a certain reckless air that was far from agreeable,—still—"

"O grandma!" interrupted Bertha, with an expression of incredulity, "it can't be possible that old Joe ever had a grain of good looks. Why! his face is actually hideous and disgusting, and so bloated that I could scarcely see his eyes; and, grandma, it was horrible, horrible! his long, yellow beard was covered with vomit, and—O grandma! how *could* he ever have been attractive?" and Bertha shuddered.

"I tell you, my dear," explained grandma, "there is nothing on earth that is so brutalizing and degrading in its effect upon the human system as strong drink. It is the devil's own weapon, and with it, he succeeds too often in bringing his poor, duped victims far below the level of the brutes.

"About this time Joe became acquainted with a beautiful young girl, the daughter of a merchant who lived in the city, where Joe now had his home.

"Meanwhile, good Aunt Maggie had died, leaving Joe the little remnant of property which she had. This was soon spent, of course, in folly and dissipation by the poor prodigal.

"But tell me about the pretty young girl," persuaded Bertha.

"Her name was Martha Grey," replied grandma, "and all too soon the reckless and dissipated young man succeeded in winning her heart, for, as I told you, he was handsome and kind-hearted; although he possessed a high opinion of his own good looks and capabilities.

"He had attended school a good deal, and was no mean student, and after a time he began the study of law. He might have succeeded well in this, his chosen profession, had he been diligent and persevering; but his old enemy, *appetite*, was constantly upon his track, and it was not long before he lost his practice, because nobody wanted to employ a drunken lawyer. After he had been seen reeling down the street a few times, he soon found himself without clients."

"But, grandma," protested Bertha, "I don't see how he could have kept all this hidden from poor Martha Grey."

"Ah, he could not,—though he tried hard enough to do so, for Mr. Grey, Martha's father, was very much opposed to strong drink. But one day Joe so

5

far forgot himself as to enter Mr. Grey's store quite
intoxicated. Of course, the merchant was very
much displeased and disgusted and forbade the

"He entered Mr. Grey's store quite intoxicated."

young man ever to visit his daughter again. Still,
I am sorry to say, Martha insisted upon meeting Joe,
and still accepted his company."

"Why didn't you go and talk with her,
grandma?" suggested Henri, "maybe you could
have persuaded her, even if her father could not;
she must have been a silly young lady, I'm sure."

"O my dear boy!" exclaimed grandma. "If you
had known Martha Grey, you could not have said
that. No; she was a beautiful girl, but a most
mistaken one," and grandma sighed. "I went to
visit her, myself, many times, and most earnestly
did I try to persuade her to quit the company of
this reckless and dissipated young man. Poor Martha's face would turn very pale as I talked with her,
but her voice was low and decided as she replied:—

"'I know you think him very bad, dear friend, but poor Joseph is not altogether so, and he has promised me to quit his cups entirely, and I am sure he will. I think it is my mission to make a

'I think it is my mission to make a good man of Joe."

good man of Joe,—to reform him, in fact, and I believe I can do it, at least, I mean to try.' So in spite of all that I could do, and in spite of the efforts of her father, and many interested friends, she ran away trom home and married the poor drunkard."

"Didn't Joe behave himself any better then?" asked Henri.

"Better?—no, no; and from that moment, the fate of the poor, mistaken girl was sealed. To be sure, her wretched husband would have periods of repenting, and spend days and nights of misery and remorse, but the demon which he had entertained and fed so many long years was not to be easily banished."

"Did Mr. Grey ever forgive his daughter and take her home again?" queried Bertha, her blue eyes full of tears, "O, I hope so, grandma."

"Mr. Grey was a kind father, and he loved his daughter very tenderly. So, after a while he went to see Joe, and invited him to take a position as clerk in his store. The poor fellow was only too glad to accept the kind offer, and promised most faithfully to reform. Of course, his devoted wife was much encouraged, and for a time all went well.

"But, my children," continued grandma, "there is nothing but the power of Christ, which can lay hold of the victim of rum, and stand him upon his feet and keep him from falling. But for this wonderful power, poor Joe had never asked.

"Still he struggled in his own strength,—struggled most pitifully, to break the strong bands which bound him,—struggled vainly as poor Samson did when he was shorn of his strength. But it was only a few weeks before poor Joe had fallen again. Some of his old companions, jealous of his success and altered circumstances, determined to compass his ruin.

"'Come in, Joe, man, come in and take a glass with your old friends,' they called one day as he was passing a saloon where he had so lately been a drunken idler. Joe had not the courage to refuse, for there was nothing so dreaded by him as to have it said that he was tied to a woman's apron string."

"O, I'm so sorry!" exclaimed Bertha, for she was a very sympathetic little girl. "Of course, the foolish man went into the saloon."

"Indeed, he did, and when he came out again, his

"Of course, the foolish man went into the saloon."

drunken legs would scarcely carry him home."

"Did his father-in-law send him away now? I'm very sure I should," reflected Max stoutly. "I would not have a drunken man about."

"I am glad to know that you hate strong drink, my lad," replied grandma, placing her hand kindly upon his head, "but we must none of us forget that Christ died for *all*, even the poor drunkard, and we should pity, and do all we can for him. Yes, Mr. Grey forgave him and took him back, not only this time, but many times afterward, until finally after a few years, his poor wife, beautiful Martha Grey, died heartbroken and wretched.

"Then Joe went away, and after a time he went to sea. Finally, after many years, he became the wretched, drunken outcast whom you saw to-day.

"Now children, I have told you the story of poor old Joe, and I want you to learn this verse, which is one of the proverbs of Solomon, the wise man :—

"'For the drunkard and the glutton shall come to poverty; and drowsiness shall clothe a man with rags.'"

LITTLE JOEY   OLD JOE

THE BEGINNING AND THE ENDING

EFFECTS OF STIMULANTS

BY MRS. E. G. WHITE

 NOW you not that they which run a race run all, but one receiveth the prize? So run, that you may obtain. And every man that striveth for the mastery is temperate in all things. Now they do it to obtain a corruptible crown; but we an incorruptible."

Here the good results of self control and temperate habits are set forth. The various games instituted among the ancient Greeks in honor of their gods, are presented before us by the apostle Paul to illustrate the spiritual warfare and its reward. Those who were to participate in these games were trained by the most severe discipline. Every indulgence that would tend to weaken the physical powers was forbidden. Luxurious food and wine were prohibited, in order to promote physical vigor, fortitude, and firmness.

To win the prize for which they strove,—a chaplet of perishable flowers, bestowed amid the applause of the multitude,—was considered the highest honor. If so much could be endured, so much self-denial practised, in the hope of gaining so worthless a prize, which only one at best could obtain, how much greater should be the sacrifice, how much

Daniel and His Fellows Refusing the King's Meat

(72)

greater should be the sacrifice, how much more willing the self-denial, for an incorruptible crown, and for everlasting life !

There is work for us to do—stern, earnest work. All our habits, tastes, and inclinations must be educated in harmony with the laws of life and health. By this means we may secure the very best physical conditions, and have mental clearness to discern between the evil and the good.

In order rightly to understand the subject of temperance, we must consider it from a Bible standpoint; and nowhere can we find a more comprehensive and forcible illustration of true temperance and its attendant blessings, than is afforded by the history of the prophet Daniel and his Hebrew associates in the court of Babylon.

When these youth were selected to be educated in the "learning and the tongue of the Chaldeans," that they might "stand in the king's palace," there was appointed them a daily allowance from the king's table, both of food and wine. "But Daniel purposed in his heart that he would not defile himself with the portion of the king's meat, nor with the wine which he drank."

The food appointed them would include meats pronounced unclean by the law of Moses. They requested the officer who had them in charge to give them a more simple fare ; but he hesitated, fearing that such rigid abstinence as they proposed would affect their personal appearance unfavorably, and bring himself into disfavor with the king. Daniel pleaded for a ten days' trial. This was granted, and at the expiration of that time these youth were found to be far more healthy in appearance than those who had partaken of the king's dainties. Hence the simple pulse and water which they at first requested, was thereafter the food of Daniel and his companions.

It was not their own pride or ambition that brought these young men into the king's court,— into the companionship of those who neither knew nor feared the true God. They were captives in a strange land, and Infinite Wisdom had placed them there. At this trial of their loyalty, they considered their position, with its dangers and difficulties, and then in the fear of God made their decision. Even at the risk of the king's displeasure, they would be true to the religion of their fathers.

They obeyed the divine law, both physical and moral, and the blessing of God gave them strength and comeliness and intellectual power.

These youth had received a right education in early life, and now, when separated from home influences and sacred associations, they honored the instructors of their childhood. With their habits of self-denial were coupled earnestness of purpose, diligence, and steadfastness. They were not actuated by pride or unworthy ambition ; but sought to acquit themselves creditably, for the honor of their down-trodden people, and for His glory whose servants they were.

When the ability and acquirements of these youth

were tested by the king at the end of the three years of training, none were found like unto Daniel, Hananiah, Mishael, and Azariah. Their keen apprehension, their choice and exact language, their extensive and varied knowledge, testified to the unimpaired strength and vigor of their mental powers. Therefore they stood before the king. "And in all matters of wisdom and understanding, that the king enquired of them, he found them ten times better than all the magicians and astrologers that were in all his realm."

God always honors the right. The most promising youth from all the lands subdued by the great conqueror had been gathered at Babylon, yet amid them all, the Hebrew captives were without a rival. The erect form, the firm, elastic step, the fair countenance, the undimmed senses, the untainted breath, —all were so many certificates of good habits,— insignia of the nobility with which nature honors those who are obedient to her laws.

The history of Daniel and his companions has been recorded on the pages of the inspired word, for the benefit of the youth of all succeeding ages. What men have done, men may do. Did those youthful Hebrews stand firm amid great temptations, and bear a noble testimony in favor of true temperance?—the youth of to-day may bear a similar testimony.

The lesson here presented is one which we would do well to ponder. Our danger is not from scarcity, but from abundance. We are constantly tempted to excess. Those who would preserve their powers unimpaired for the service of God, must observe strict temperance in the use of His bounties, as well as total abstinence from every injurious or debasing indulgence.

The rising generation are surrounded by allurements calculated to tempt the appetite. Especially in our large cities, every form of indulgence is made easy and inviting. Those who, like Daniel, refuse to defile themselves, will reap the reward of their temperate habits. With their greater physical stamina and increased power of endurance, they have a bank of desposit on which to draw in case of emergency.

Right physical habits promote mental superiority. Intellectual power, physical strength, and longevity depend upon immutable laws. There is no happen-so, no chance, about this matter. Nature's God will not interfere to preserve men from the consequences of violating nature's laws. There is much sterling truth in the adage, "Every man is the architect of his own fortune." While parents are responsible for the stamp of character, as well as for the education and training, of their sons and daughters, it is still true that our position and usefulness in the world depend, to a great degree, upon our own course of action. Daniel and his companions enjoyed the benefits of correct training and education in early life, but these advantages alone would not have made them what they were. The time came when they must act for themselves,—

when their future depended upon their own course. Then they decided to be true to the lessons given them in childhood. The fear of God, which is the beginning of wisdom, was the foundation of their greatness. His Spirit strengthened every true purpose, every noble resolution.

Intemperance has cursed the world almost from its infancy. Noah's son was so debased by the excessive use of wine, that he lost all sense of propriety, and the curse which followed his sin has never been lifted from his descendants.

Nadab and Abihu were men in holy office; but by the use of wine, their minds became so clouded that they could not distinguish between sacred and common things. By the offering of "strange fire" they disregarded God's command, and were slain by His judgments.

Alexander found it much easier to subdue kingdoms than to rule his own spirit. After conquering nations, this so-called great man fell, through the indulgence of appetite—a victim of intemperance.

Notwithstanding thousands of years of experience and progress, the same dark blot which stained the pages of history, remains to disfigure our modern civilization. Drunkenness, with all its woes, is found everywhere we go. In spite of the noble efforts of temperance workers, the evil has gained ground. License laws have been enacted, but legal regulation has not stayed its progress, except in comparitively limited territory. Efforts have been made to establish institutions where the victims of intemperance might receive help to overcome their terrible appetite. This is a noble work, but how much wiser, how much more effective, would have been the removal of the cause of all this woe! Considering only the financial aspect of this question, what folly it is to tolerate a business that is making paupers by the thousand! The laws of the land legalize the trade of making drunkards, and then at great expense, provide institutions for converting them again into sober men! Can our legislators furnish no better solution of the liquor question?

So long as the sale of liquor is sanctioned by law, the victims of appetite can receive but little benefit through inebriate asylums. They cannot remain there always; they must again take their place in society. The appetite for intoxicating drinks, though it may be subdued, is not wholly destroyed, and when temptation assails them, as it must on every hand, they too often fall an easy prey.

What can be done to press back this inflowing tide of evil? Let laws be enacted and rigidly enforced prohibiting the sale and use of ardent spirits. Let every effort be made to encourage the inebriate's return to temperance and virtue. But even more than this is needed to banish the curse of inebriety from our land. Let the appetite for intoxicating liquors be removed, and the demand for them is at an end.

Only men of strict temperance and integrity should be admitted to our legislative halls, or chosen to preside in our courts of justice. Property, reputation, and even life itself, are insecure when left to the judgment of men who are intemperate and immoral. How many innocent persons have been condemned to death, how many more have been robbed of all their earthly possessions, by the injustice of drinking jurors, lawyers, witnesses, and even judges!

There is need now of men like Daniel, to do and dare. A pure heart and a strong, fearless hand are wanted in the world to-day. God designed that man should be constantly improving,—daily reaching a higher point in the scale of excellence. He will help us, if we help ourselves. It is the duty of every Christian to see that his example and influence are on the side of reform. Let ministers of the gospel lift up their voices like a trumpet, and show the people their transgression, and the house of Israel their sins. The youth need to be instructed. Our hope of happiness in two worlds depends upon our improvement of one. We should be guarded at every point against the first approach to intemperance. If we would preserve our children from evil, we must give them a right example, and then teach them to make God their fear, their wisdom, and their strength.

The use of intoxicating liquor dethrones reason, and hardens the heart against every pure and holy influence. The inanimate rocks will sooner listen to the appeals of truth and justice, than will that man whose sensibilities are paralyzed by intemperance. Those who venture to enter the forbidden path are gradually and unconsciously led on, until they become demoralized, corrupted, and maddened. And while Christians are asleep, this evil is gaining more strength and making fresh victims. If the moral sensibilities of Christians were aroused upon the subject of temperance in *all things*, and they realized that the final destiny of every one depends upon the habits he forms, they could by their example, help those who are weak in self-control, to resist the cravings of appetite.

We witness great struggles in our country to put down intemperance; but it is a hard matter to over-come and chain a full-grown lion. If half the efforts that have been put forth to stay this giant evil, had been directed toward enlightening parents in regard to their responsibility in forming the habits and character of their children, a thousand-fold more good might have resulted. The unnatural appetite for spirituous liquors is often created at home, in many cases at the tables of the very ones who are most zealous to lead out in the temperance work. We bid all workers Godspeed; but we invite them to look more deeply into the cause of the evil they war against, and to be more thorough and consist-ent in reform.

Through the intemperance begun at home, the digestive organs first become weakened, and soon ordinary food does not satisfy the appetite. Un-healthful conditions are established, and there is a craving for more stimulating food. Tea and coffee produce an immediate effect. Under the influence of these poisons the nervous system is excited, and in some cases, for the time being, the intellect seems to be invigorated, the imagination more vivid.

Because these stimulants produce such agreeable results, many conclude that they really need them; but there is always a reaction. The nervous system has borrowed power from its future resources, for present use, and all this temporary invigoration is followed by corresponding depression. The suddenness of the relief obtained from tea and coffee, is an evidence that what seems to be strength is only nervous excitement, and consequently must be an injury to the system.

The appetite thus educated continually to crave something stronger, demands an increase of the agreeable excitement. Its demands become more frequent, and more difficult to control. The more debilitated the system and the less able to do without unnatural stimulus, the more the desire for these things increases, until the will is overborne, and there seems to be no power to deny the unnatural craving.

When there has been a departure from the right path, it is difficult to return. Barriers have been broken down, safeguards removed. One step in the wrong direction prepares the way for another. The least deviation from right principles will lead to separation from God, and may end in destruction. What we do once, we more readily do again; and to go forward in a certain path, be it right or

6

wrong, is more easy than to start. To corrupt our ways before God requires no effort; but to ingraft habits of righteousness and truth upon the character takes time and patient endeavor.

Many who would hesitate to place liquor to a neighbor's lips, will engage in the raising of hops, and thus lend their influence against the temperance cause. I cannot see how, in the light of the law of God, Christians can conscientiously engage in the raising of hops or the manufacture of wine and cider for the market.

I have often heard people say, "Oh! this is only sweet cider. It is perfectly harmless, and even healthful." Several quarts, perhaps gallons, are carried home. For a short time it is sweet; then fermentation begins. The sharp taste makes it all the more acceptable to many palates, and the lover of sweet wine and cider is loath to admit that his favorite beverage ever becomes hard and sour.

Intoxication is just as really produced by wine and cider as by stronger drinks, and it is the worst kind of inebriation. The passions are more perverse; the transformation of character is greater, more determined, and obstinate. A few quarts of cider or wine may awaken a taste for stronger drinks, and in many cases those who have become confirmed drunkards have thus laid the foundation of the drinking habit.

For persons who have inherited an appetite for stimulants, it is by no means safe to have wine or cider in the house; for Satan is continually soliciting them to indulge. If they yield to his temptations, they do not know where to stop; appetite clamors for indulgence, and is gratified to their ruin. The brain is clouded; reason no longer holds the reins, but lays them on the neck of lust. Licentiousness abounds, and vices of almost every type are practiced as the result of indulging the appetite for wine and cider. It is impossible for one who loves these stimulants, and accustoms himself to their use, to grow in grace. He becomes gross and sensual; the animal passions control the higher powers of the mind, and virtue is not cherished.

Moderate drinking is the school in which men are receiving an education for the drunkard's career. So gradually does Satan lead away from the strongholds of temperance, so insidiously do wine and cider exert their influence upon the taste, that the highway to drunkenness is entered upon all unsuspectingly. The taste for stimulants is cultivated; the nervous system is disordered; Satan keeps the mind in a fever of unrest, and the poor victim, imagining himself perfectly secure, goes on and on, until every barrier is broken down, every principle sacrificed. The strongest resolutions are undermined, and eternal interests are too weak to keep the debased appetite under the control of reason. Some are never really drunk, but are always under the influence of mild intoxicants. They are feverish, unstable in mind, not really delirious, but as truly unbalanced; for the nobler powers of the mind are perverted.

Wherever we go, we encounter the tobacco devotee, enfeebling both mind and body by his darling
indulgence. Have men a right to deprive their
Maker and the world of the service which is their
due? Tobacco is a slow, insidious poison. Its
effects are more difficult to erase from the system
than are those of liquor. It binds the victim in
even stronger bands of slavery than does the intoxicating cup. It is a disgusting habit, defiling to
the user, and very annoying to others. We rarely
pass through a crowd, but men will puff their poisoned breath in our faces. It is unpleasant, if not
dangerous, to remain in a railway car or in a room
where the atmosphere is impregnated with the fumes
of liquor and tobacco. Is it honorable thus to con-
taminate the air which others must breathe?

What power can the tobacco devotee have to stay
the progress of intemperance? There must be a
revolution upon the subject of tobacco before the
ax will be laid at the root of the tree. Tea, coffee,
and tobacco, as well as alcoholic drinks, are different degrees in the scale of artificial stimulants.

The effect of tea and coffee, as heretofore shown,
tends in the same direction as that of wine and
cider, liquor and tobacco.

Tea is a stimulant, and to a certain extent produces intoxication. It gradually impairs the energy
of body and mind. Its first effect is exhilarating,
because it quickens the motions of the living
machinery; and the tea drinker thinks that it is
doing him great service. But this is a mistake.

When its influence is gone, the unnatural force abates, and the result is languor and debility corresponding to the artificial vivacity imparted. The second effect of tea drinking is headache, wakefulness, palpitation of the heart, indigestion, trembling, and many other evils.

Coffee is a hurtful indulgence. It temporarily excites the mind to unwonted action, but the aftereffect is exhaustion, prostration, paralysis of the mental, moral, and physical powers. The mind becomes enervated, and unless through determined effort the habit is overcome, the activity of the brain is permanently lessened.

All these nerve irritants are wearing away the life forces, and the restlessness caused by shattered nerves, the impatience, the mental feebleness, become warring elements, antagonizing to spiritual progress. Then should not those who advocate temperance and reform be awake to counteract the evils of these injurious drinks? In some cases it is as difficult to break up the tea-and-coffee habit as it is for the inebriate to discontinue the use of liquor. The money expended for tea and coffee is worse than wasted. They do the user only harm, and that continually. Those who use tea, coffee, opium, and alcohol, may sometimes live to old age, but this fact is no argument in favor of the use of these stimulants. What these persons might have accomplished, but failed to, because of their intemperate habits, the great day of God alone will reveal.

Those who resort to tea and coffee for stimulation to labor, will feel the evil effects of this course in trembling nerves and lack of self-control. Tired nerves need rest and quiet. Nature needs time to recuperate her exhausted energies. But if her forces are goaded on by the use of stimulants, there is, whenever this process is repeated, a lessening of real force. For a time, more may be accomplished under the unnatural stimulus, but gradually it becomes more difficult to rouse the energies to the desired point, and at last exhausted nature can no longer respond.

The habit of drinking coffee and tea is a greater evil than is often suspected. Many who have accustomed themselves to the use of stimulating drinks, suffer from headache and nervous prostration, and lose much time on account of sickness. They imagine they cannot live without the stimulus, and are ignorant of its effect upon the health. What makes it more dangerous is, that its evil effects are so often attributed to other causes.

Through the use of stimulants, the whole system suffers. The nerves are unbalanced, the liver is morbid in its action, the quality and circulation of the blood are affected, and the skin becomes inactive and sallow. The mind, too, is injured. The immediate influence of these stimulants is to excite the brain to undue activity, only to leave it weaker and less capable of exertion. The after-effect is prostration, not only mental and physical, but moral. As a result we see nervous men and women, of unsound judgment and unbalanced mind. They often manifest a hasty, impatient, accusing spirit, viewing the faults of others as through a magnifying glass, and utterly unable to discern their own defects.

When these tea and coffee users meet together for social entertainment, the effects of their pernicious habit are manifest. All partake freely of the favorite beverages, and as the stimulating influence is felt, their tongues are loosened, and they begin the wicked work of talking against others. Their words are not few or well chosen. The tidbits of gossip are passed around, too often the poison of scandal as well. These thoughtless gossipers forget that they have a witness. An unseen Watcher is writing their words in the books of heaven. All these unkind criticisms, these exaggerated reports, these envious feelings, expressed under the excitement of the cup of tea, Jesus registers as against Himself. "Inasmuch as ye have done it unto one of the least of these my brethren, ye have done it unto Me."

We are already suffering because of the wrong habits of our fathers, and yet how many take a course in every way worse than theirs! Opium, tea, coffee, tobacco, and liquor are rapidly extinguishing the spark of vitality still left in the race. Every year millions of gallons of intoxicating liquors are drank, and millions of dollars are spent for tobacco. And the slaves of appetite, while constantly spending their earnings in sensual indulgence, rob their children of food and clothing and

(88)   *Tea Table Gossips*

the advantages of education. There can never be a right state of society while these evils exist.

When the appetite for spirituous liquor is indulged, the man voluntarily places to his lips the draught which debases below the level of the brute, him who was made in the image of God. Reason is paralyzed, the intellect is benumbed, the animal passion is excited, and then follow crimes of the most debasing character. How can the user of rum and tobacco give to God an undivided heart?—It is impossible. Neither can he love his neighbor as himself. The darling indulgence engrosses all his affections. To gratify his craving for strong drink, he sells reason and self-control. He places to his lips that which stupefies the brain, paralyzes the intellect, and makes him a shame and a curse to his family, and a terror to all around him. If men would become temperate in all things, if they would touch not, taste not, handle not, tea, coffee, tobacco, wines, opium, and alcoholic drinks, reason would take the reins of government in her own hands, and hold the appetite and passions under control.

Through appetite, Satan controls the mind and the whole being. Thousands who might have lived have passed to the grave, physical, mental, and moral wrecks, because they sacrificed all their powers to the indulgence of appetite. The necessity for the men of this generation to call to their aid the power of the will, strengthened by the grace of God, in order to withstand the temptations of Satan, and resist the least indulgence of perverted

appetite, is far greater than it was several genera-
tions ago. But the present generation have less
power of self-control than had those who lived then.
Those who indulged in these stimulants transmitted
their depraved appetites and passions to their children, and greater moral power is now required to
resist intemperance in all its forms. The only perfectly safe course is to stand firm, observing strict
temperance in all things, and never venturing into
the path of danger.

I feel an intense interest that fathers and mothers
should realize the solemn obligations that are resting upon them at this time. We are bringing up
children who will be controlled by the power of
Satan or by that of Christ. The only way in which
any can be secure against the power of intemperance, is to abstain wholly from wine, beer, and
strong drinks. We must teach our children that in
order to be manly, they must let these things alone.
God has shown us what constitutes true manliness.
It is he that overcometh who will be honored, and
whose name will not be blotted out of the book of life.

When the Lord would raise up Samson as a de-
liverer of His people, He enjoined upon the mother
correct habits of life before the birth of her child.
And the same prohibition was to be imposed, from
the first, upon the child; for he was to be conse-
crated to God as a Nazarite from his birth.

The angel of God appeared to the wife of Manoah,
and informed her that she should have a son; and
in view of this, he gave her the important directions:

"Now therefore beware, I pray thee, and drink not wine nor strong drink, and eat not any unclean thing."

God had important work for the promised child of Manoah to do, and it was to secure for him the qualifications necessary for this work, that the habits of both the mother and the child were to be so carefully regulated. "Neither let her drink wine nor strong drink," was the angel's instruction for the wife of Manoah, "nor eat any unclean thing: all that I commanded her let her observe." The child will be affected for good or evil by the habits of the mother. She must herself be controlled by principle, and must practice temperance and self-denial, if she would seek the welfare of her child.

In the New Testament we find a no less impressive example of the importance of temperate habits.

John the Baptist was a reformer. To him was committed a great work for the people of his time. And in preparation for that work, all his habits were carefully regulated, even from his birth. The angel Gabriel was sent from heaven to instruct the parents of John in the principles of health reform. He "shall drink neither wine nor strong drink," said the heavenly messenger; "and he shall be filled with the Holy Ghost."

John separated himself from his friends, and from the luxuries of life, dwelling alone in the wilderness, and subsisting on a purely vegetable diet. The simplicity of his dress—a garment woven of camel's hair—was a rebuke to the extravagance

1 Samuel Presented to Eli   2 Samson and the Gate of Gaza
(92)   3 John the Baptist in the Wilderness

and display of the people of his generation, especially of the Jewish priests. His diet also, of locusts and wild honey, was a rebuke to the gluttony that everywhere prevailed.

The work of John was foretold by the prophet Malachi: "Behold, I will send you Elijah the prophet before the coming of the great and dreadful day of the Lord; and he shall turn the heart of the fathers to the children, and the heart of the children to their fathers." John the Baptist went forth in the spirit and power of Elijah, to prepare the way of the Lord, and to turn the people to the wisdom of the just. He was a representative of those living in the last days, to whom God has entrusted sacred truths to present before the people, to prepare the way for the second coming of Christ. And the same principles of temperance which John practiced should be observed by those who in our day are to warn the world of the coming of the Son of man.

God has made man in His own image, and He expects man to preserve unimpaired the powers that have been imparted to him for the Creator's service. Then should we not heed His admonitions, and seek to preserve every power in the best condition to serve him? The very best we can give to God is feeble enough.

Why is there so much misery in the world to-day? Is it because God loves to see His creatures suffer?— O no! it is because men become weakened by immoral practices. We mourn over Adam's transgression, and seem to think that our first parents showed great weakness in yielding to temptation; but if Adam's transgression were the only evil we had to meet, the condition of the world would be much better than it is. There has been a succession of falls since Adam's day.

Indulgence in spirituous liquors is causing great wretchedness in the world. Though liquor drinkers are told again and again that they are shortening their life, they still go on in transgression. Why not cease to break the laws of God? Why not seek to preserve themselves in a condition of health? This is what God requires of them. If Christians would bring all their appetites and passions under the control of enlightened conscience, feeling it a duty they owe to God and to their neighbor to obey the laws which govern life and health, they would have the blessing of physical and mental vigor; they would have moral power to engage in the warfare against Satan; and in the name of Him who conquered in their behalf, they might be more than conquerors on their own account.

All around us are the victims of depraved appetite, and what are you going to do for them? Can you not, by your example, help them to place their feet in the path of temperance? Can you have a sense of the temptations that are coming upon the youth who are growing up around us, and not seek to warn and save them? Who will stand on the Lord's side? Who will help to press back this tide of immorality, of woe, and wretchedness, that is filling the world? We entreat of you to turn your attention to the work of overcoming. Those who shall at last have a right to the tree of life, will be those who have kept God's commandments.

It is not an easy matter to overcome the appetite for narcotics and stimulants. But in the name of Christ this great victory can be gained. His love for the fallen race was so great that He made an infinite sacrifice to reach them in their degradation and through His divine power finally elevate them to His throne. But it rests with man whether Christ shall accomplish for him that which He is fully able to do. God cannot work against man's will to save him from Satan's artifices. Man must put forth his human power to resist and conquer at any cost; he must be a co-worker with Christ. Then, through the victory that it is his privilege to gain by the all-powerful name of Jesus, he may become an heir of God, and a partaker with Christ of His glory. No drunkard can inherit the kingdom of God; but "to him that overcometh will I grant to sit with Me in My throne, even as I also overcame, and am set down with My Father in His throne."

UNCLE BEN'S STORY

HAVE a good mind to tell you a story," said Uncle Ben, drawing his chair a little nearer the smiling group of young people which surrounded the table in the sitting room.

"Do, Uncle Ben," they replied.

As Uncle Ben announced his intention of telling a story, all eyes were turned upon him. Mother laid aside her book and spectacles, and father leaned back in his easy chair to listen, for Uncle Ben's stories were always worth hearing.

As uncle spoke, we wondered that he looked so sad. Placing his feet upon a footstool, he began:—

"Many years ago, after I had graduated at college, I had a strong desire for a situation on one of the railways that was then being built through the United States. Through the influence of my friends, I received a position as fireman on one of the leading roads.

"I soon won the esteem and good will of all of the officers and employees on the road. As time passed, the superintendent and I became deeply attached to each other. We were about the same age. There is nothing I would not do for Frank Benway. I realized the duties of my position and determined to discharge them honorably.

"But I was led away,—led down, down, where so many have gone before and since. I was induced by thoughtless associates to drink. One evening I had drunk more than usual, when Frank Benway came in. I did not see him until he touched me on the arm.

"'Ben,' said he, 'come away! for my sake, come away.'

"He took my arm and led me out into the cool, night air. When he spoke again, it was in a pleading, sorrowful tone.

"'Ben, for the sake of your mother, for the sake of the friendship between us, never drink again. Good night, my dear friend.'

"I went to my lodgings with a dizzy head and a heavy heart. I knew that my friend ought to turn me away from my situation, but he was too kindhearted, and had too much confidence in me, even yet, to do that. (I knew that he fully expected that I would heed his earnest entreaty.)

"But when I awoke the next morning, I again felt the strong thirst for liquor. In one of my pockets I found a flask, filled with brandy which I had procured the night before. I had started down the hill, and thought I could not resist the temptation to take just one more drink,— *just one more.*

"The Superintendent had

"Just one more drink"

gone down the road on an express train, early that morning, as there were some repairs to be made part way down the line, which he wished to superintend personally.

"Our train started in about an hour after the express. The engineer of the train had been detained at the other end of the road on account of sickness. I was alone on the engine, but the conductor had perfect confidence in my ability.

"I had never drunk enough to become intoxicated before, and no one on the train suspected that I had formed the fatal habit. I still continued to drink until I became so helpless I could not stand, and this was after I had taken my place in the cab of the engine.

"I fell against the tender soon after we got under way, and cut a severe gash in my forehead. I attempted to rise, but could not. My senses were clear, however, and I knew all that was passing with horrible reality.

"I had fallen in such a position that I could see out at one side between the tender and the engine. On, on we swept at lightning speed, with no hand to guide the train or to regulate its speed.

"We had just passed the point where they were making the repairs I spoke of, when, as we swept around a little bend in the road, I saw Frank Benway, a few rods ahead of us, walking swiftly up the track. Suddenly I saw him step upon a bit of stone which lay there, and, slipping, his foot was caught between the ground and the rail.

"O how he struggled to rise, but could not! On

we rushed. My poor friend's pitiful efforts to rise were in vain. And it is still the bitterest moment of my life that at that moment I was too intoxicated to reverse the engine, which I might have done, probably in time to have saved his life!

"There I lay, bound by the horrible chains which I had forged for myself. I could not move! Frank saw me, for he had fallen across the track on the side where I lay on the cab floor. He held out both hands to me, as if to say: 'Help me, Ben, help me'!

"In another moment I was so near that I could look into his eyes, and the next, they were closed forever. A brakeman who saw Frank when we passed over him, now rushed to the engine, and finding me lying disgracefully stupid, I suppose divined it all. He stopped the train.

"Frank's remains were gathered up, and I was taken to my home, a raving maniac. None on the train save this brakeman suspected I had been drunk. He kept my secret— why I never knew. Perhaps he thought I was punished enough. I was ill with brain fever for a long time.

"After I recovered, I *never* tasted another drop of liquor. It seemed as if I was more than a murderer. Afterward, when I went on the road again, I was a changed man. I gradually worked myself up until I became president of that road.

"Young friends, when you pass out from your parents' care, there will be many temptations to allure you. Then, I trust, you will bear in mind the evening when you heard Uncle Ben's sad story, told *in the twilight* of his life."

JACOB BELL'S VOW

OOD-BY, Jim Brown, you have got the last cent of my money that you will ever get," said a poor, miserable looking wretch, as he turned to leave the bar-room of a hotel, where a large company of men sat drinking and carousing.

"I guess when you find a few cents, I shall get them, Jake," answered the besotted landlord with a sneer, "but I tell you again that you will get no more drinks of me until you pay off the old debt."

"Good-by, Jim Brown," said old Jake again, "you will never get one cent of it, nor will you ever sell me another glass of strong drink."

"Goin' to sign the pledge, Jake?" queried another voice, "guess 'twill not do you much good if you do, for you like rum too well to keep it long."

"Maybe I shall sign the pledge," was the reply, "but I consider my word here, just as sacred and binding as a written pledge, and so I solemnly swear before God and man never to touch another drop of the accursed poison so long as I live," and Jake retreated toward the door as he said it.

"Hold on, Jake, don't go yet," called out another voice, "come back and I will treat you. Here, landlord, give him a good glass of whiskey to make him better natured." But Jake never looked toward

the speaker, and still kept moving slowly toward
the door.

"You will try in vain, I guess," he slowly said,
"for I have drunk my last glass of liquor, God
helping me,"
and old Jake
Bell walked
away.

"Wonder
what has got
into the old
fool," said one
of the bar-room
loungers, "for I
never knew him
to refuse a glass
of whiskey be-
fore."

"Guess he'll
come back be-
fore many days

"I have drunk my last glass of liquor"

go by," was heard from another part of the room.

"Suppose that old Jake should reform," said one
who had not spoken before, "I never saw him with
such a fit on, and if he should stick to what he
said, Landlord Brown has lost one of his best customers."

"And a few shillings besides," chimed in another voice.

"Guess he has not lost much by old Jake Bell,
for if I'm not mistaken, his money has been quite

an advantage to Jim Brown for a number of years," was the reply.

"Stop your noise, will you?" said the landlord, with a scowl on his face, "I'll take care of old Jake."

"Perhaps he'll take care of himself," was his reply, "and I think he would do quite as well, and his wife and children would be the gainers."

"Stop your infernal noise, Bill Gray, or leave the room," yelled the landlord, growing black with passion.

"If I do go," said Bill quietly, "I shall go as old Jake did, never to come back again. You know that what Bill Gray says, he means."

———

Susan Bell sat by the low window of her house, looking out upon the beautiful landscape, bathed with the golden rays of the setting sun. There was an expression of pain and sadness upon her face, and occasionally a tear gleamed in her faded eyes.

We doubt if the glory of the fields and the sky had awakened one cheerful thought in her heart, and if it did, the dark clouds of misery soon turned the ray of sunlight to gloom again. Ah! the bright hopes of other days had long ago died out from the heart of Susan Bell, and the gray shadows of wretchedness had long thronged her pathway.

But the time had been when this wretched woman had seen bright days of happiness, though they appeared now like some fairy dream, which cast its mocking glory upon the barren wastes of life.

Strong drink had destroyed the hopes of poor Susan Bell, and driven peace and plenty away from the once cheerful fireside. It had ruined the prospects of Jacob Bell, and made him a miserable, besotted wretch. In other days he had been loved and respected, for he possessed many noble, generous qualities, and he seemed likely to become a man of more than ordinary usefulness in the world.

But he became possessed with a thirst for strong drink, and so started upon the fearful road of sin and ruin. His children once made music in their home, but after he began his career of sin and shame, disease laid its hand upon two of them, and they died.

Mrs. Bell did not murmur as the death angel claimed them, for she saw the storm that was gathering. It came all too soon, and then she thanked God that there were only two children left to suffer the abuse of a drunken father and to bear the heavy load of want and poverty. Jim Brown had taken the earnings of the husband and father for many years, and in return, gave him the deadly poison that made him a brute and deadened every impulse of nobleness.

"He has gone to Brown's, as usual," said Susan Bell to herself. "Oh, how I wish that he would not go there so often! He will never even try to reform as long as he goes there to spend his leisure hours."

A tear dropped from her eyes as she looked in the direction of the village tavern. "It will do no good to hope any longer, for he will never do any better," she said half aloud.

The sun went down behind the western mountain and twilight began to gather over the earth. Still Susan Bell sat by the low window, looking toward the now lighted bar-room. "Why! he is coming!" she exclaimed, as she saw the well known form of her husband, coming down the street, in the twilight. "How strange that Jacob should come home so early; I wonder what it means."

Jacob walked steadily into the house, and in a

" Susan Bell sat by the low window"

pleasant voice asked: "Susan, will you get some supper? I am very hungry."

"We have but little to eat, Jacob," was the reply, "but I will get you what we have."

"Have we any coffee?"

"No, but perhaps I can borrow a little of Mrs. Blake."

"Have we any flour or sugar, Susan," was the next inquiry.

"None," was the reply.

"Then I will go and buy some," said Jacob. "Mr. Grant is owing me for a half day's work, and I guess he can pay me."

"Susan Bell's heart beat very fast as her husband started out again. "Oh, if he does not stop at Brown's!" she exclaimed to herself.

He did not stop at Brown's, although a dozen voices called to him as he was passing by. "I think you will not succeed," he said quietly, as he walked toward home.

"Now, make me a cup of coffee, Susan," he said, as he placed several small packages upon the table.

His wife quickly obeyed, and in a short time Jacob sat down to a better supper than he had had for many a day.

"I am very tired to-night," he said, as he finished the meal, "but please call me early in the morning, Susan, for I am going to work for Mr. Grant. I have taken the job of building his barn, and want to get it well started this week."

Mrs. Bell could scarcely sleep that night; there was a strange, deep joy in her heart, that she had not known for years. And yet, she hardly dared to hope. She really could not account for the strange conduct of her husband.

The day came with its beautiful splendor, and just as the morning sun began to bathe the far away mountains with light, Jacob Bell sat down to his morning meal.

After breakfast, he asked: "Have you enough flour to last to-day?"

"We have a little," was the reply.

The day passed away at last, and just as the sun was setting, Jacob Bell entered the door of his home.

"Here are three dollars, Susan," he said. "Take the money and use it as you think best. Herbert can bring home whatever you like, for he will not work any longer for Mr. Hill. He is not strong enough to do such work as he has been in the habit of doing there. He will go to school the remainder of the summer."

Mrs. Bell said not a word. She only hoped and prayed.

Another day passed away and three dollars more were placed in her hands. A whole week went by, and her husband had worked every day, and had not once visited Jim Brown's saloon.

"*Here are three dollars*"

Then he came home one night with a new suit of clothes.

"These were a present to me," he said simply, in reply to Susan's inquiry. "Mr. Grant gave them to me."

"And why did he do it, Jacob?" asked Susan in a trembling voice.

"If I tell you, then you will know my secret. But I think I will. It was because I signed the pledge."

"Have you signed the pledge, Jacob?" asked the wife in a voice choked with emotion.

"Yes," he quietly answered, "and with God's help, I will keep it. Jim brown has got the last cent of my money that he will ever get."

"Why did you take this step?" Susan asked, trying very hard to keep her voice from trembling.

"I can't really tell you, Susan, but Mr. Grant, I think, was the true cause of it. He has talked so earnestly and kindly to me of late, that I saw myself as I never did before.

"And then about a week ago, I went to Jim Brown's bar-room and asked him to trust me for a drink. I was owing him a few shillings, and as he was nearly drunk himself, he refused to trust me. I was very angry; and then I made a vow before all present never to drink another drop of liquor, and as I have said before, God helping me, I will never taste that accursed poison again."

Susan Bell silently thanked God, and earnestly prayed that he would help her husband to keep his vow sacredly.

Five years have passed away with their sunshine and shadow, and still Jacob Bell keeps his vow. The old brown house has been transformed by his skillful hand, and it is the prettiest cottage in the village. Everything about the place betokens thrift and plenty.

Jacob Bell looks much younger than he did five years ago, and for some reason, people do not call him "Old Jake." The village travern still stands, but old Jim Brown died long ago with delirium tremens. Another rum seller fills his place, but Jacob Bell has never spoken to him.

Thus did the drunkard keep his vow.

"Who hath woe? who hath sorrow? who hath contentions? who hath babbling? who hath wounds without cause? who hath redness of eyes?—They that tarry long at the wine; they that go to seek mixed wine.

"Look not thou upon the wine when it is red, when it giveth his color in the cup, when it moveth itself aright. At the last it biteth like a serpent, and stingeth like an adder."—*Solomon*.

"Every man that striveth for the mastery is temperate in all things."—*Paul*.

TESTIMONY OF RELIGIOUS BODIES

"We hold that the proper attitude of Christians toward this [liquor] traffic, is one of uncompromising opposition."— *General Conference of the Methodist Episcopal Church at Philadelphia, Pa., 1884.*

"That curse of our race—alcohol . . . the enemy alike of God and man."— *Methodist Episcopal Church, South, General Conierence, 1883.*

"The giant evil of the age—the curse of curses." — *Cumberland Presbyterian Church, General Assembly at Lebanon, Tenn., May, 1878.*

"There can be no compromise with this evil [liquor traffic]."— *United Presbyterian Church Assembly, 1885.*

"Nearly allied to theft and robbery, and in its consequences far exceeds them in enormity." – *Free Baptist Church, General Confereuce, Fairport, N. Y., 1853.*

"Opposed to *all traffic* in intoxicating drinks." —*Moravian Church, Synod of 1873.*

"Utterly inconsistent with the character and profession of members of the church of Christ to encourage in any way the traffic in intoxicating liquors."— *Reformed Dutch Church, General Synod, at Syracuse, N. Y., June, 1885.*

"The enemy of religion, of good morals, and of the best interests of our race."—*Lutheran Church, General Synod, 1879.*

ONLY A GLASS OF BEER

BOYS, did you ever stop to think that it is always the first wrong step that leads to misery and disgrace? The first petty theft leads to the penitentiary, and the first glass to the gutter, and finally to the drunkard's grave.

None who had ever known Robert Morris in his brilliant young manhood, could have dreamed of the awful fate which would finally be his. Robert was uncommonly apt in his studies, kind and courteous in his manners, and gentlemanly in appearance. He had the advantage of having been raised in a home of refinement and temperance.

But in an evil hour, he formed the acquaintance of a young man of bad principles and reckless life. For some time Robert's high sense of honor triumphed. But he could not endure the ridicule of his friend : —

"What a fool you are, Rob, old boy; come, sir, I didn't think you were such a coward ! ha ! ha ! afraid of a glass of beer !"

"I'm not afraid, Jack Horton, and I'm no coward." The next moment, and for the first time in his life, a glass of beer was pressed to his lips.

But it was by no means the last. Little by little a craving was developed for the poison—a burning thirst. His loving friends did everything in their power to rescue him. But his eyes became blood-shot, his hair unkempt, his body bloated, and his once fine intellect, like his body, defaced and ruined. Finally, after a short career of vice and folly, we followed him to an unhonored grave. His aged father groaned in agony; while the fainting form of his gray-haired mother was borne by kind hands away from the last resting place of her son.

My boy, remember that if you do not allow the first glass of liquor to pass your lips, you will never become that horrible thing—that blot on the fair creation of God—a drunkard. Do not forget that at last "it biteth like a serpent," and that "no drunkard shall inherit the kingdom of God."

IMPORTANT TESTIMONY

Wine is a mocker.—*Solomon.*

A curse.—*Queen Victoria.*

A scandal and a shame.—*Wm. E. Gladstone.*

A trap for workingmen.—*Earl Cairnes.*

Stupefies and besots.—*Bismarck*

The devil in solution.—*Sir Wilfred Lawson.*

Liquid fire and distilled damnation.—*Robert Hall.*

The mother of want and the nurse of crime.—*Lord Brougham.*

Drunkenness is the ripe fruit of moderate drinking.—*Frances E. Willard.*

ALCOHOL A CAUSE OF DISEASE

"A FOE more dreadful or deadly than the Russian or the plague."—*Florence Nightingale, from the "Crimea."*

"Most diseases have their rise in intemperance." —*Lord Bacon.*

"An active and powerful cause of disease."— *Prof. Youmans.*

"The evils of alcohol are wide-spread and countless."—*C. R. Agnew, M. D.*

"Sooner or later proves injurious to the human constitution without any exception."— *Sir B. Brodie, Sir James Clark, Sir J. Eyre, Dr. Marshall Hall, Dr. A. T. Thompson, Dr. A. Ure, the Queen's Physicians, and seventy-eight leaders in Medicine and Surgery, of England, 1839.*

"Alcohol is neither a food nor a drink suitable for his [man's] natural demands."—*B. W. Richardson, M. A., M. D., F. R. S.*

"If alcohol were unknown, half the sin and a large part of the poverty and unhappiness would disappear from the world."—*Edmond W. Parkes, M. D., F. R. S.*

"The curse of an army is intoxicating liquors." —*Parkes.*

"Injurious to health, destructive to life."— *Kant.*

"Has inflicted greater calamities than war, pestilence, and famine."— *Gladstone.*

TURNING OVER A NEW LEAF

TIS a shame!" said Mrs. Fogg, as she hurried away after the funeral of Mrs. Grant, escaping from the poor, desolate room, where two children, hardly more than babes, were sleeping, unconscious that they were motherless. "'Tis a shame that nobody'll take them."

"Yes—a bitter shame!" replied a neighbor, who was also getting off as fast as she could, so as to shift the responsibility onto some other shoulders.

"There's Mrs. Grove. She might take them as well as not. But they'll go to the poorhouse, for all she cares."

"Well, somebody'll have to answer for it," said Mrs. Fogg. "As for me, I've got youngones enough of my own."

"We left Mrs. Cole in the room. She has only one child, and her husband is well to do. I can't believe she'll have the heart to turn away from them."

"She's got the heart for anything. But we'll see."

Mrs. Cole did turn away from the sleeping babes, sighing very loud, that others might hear

8

and give her credit for a sympathy and concern she did not feel.

At last all were gone—all but a man named John Wheaton, and a poor woman, not able to take care of herself.

"What's to become of these children?" questioned Mr. Wheaton.

"Don't know. Poorhouse, I s'pose," answered the woman.

"Poorhouse?"

"Yes, nobody wants them, and there's no other place for them."

"Mamma! mamma!" cried a plaintive voice, and a flaxen-haired child, not more than two year old, rose up in the bed and looked piteously about the room. "I want my mamma!"

A great, choking sob came into the man's throat. Then the other child awoke:—

"Don't cry, sissy—mamma's gone away." At this, the little one began crying bitterly.

"I can't stand this nohow!" exclaimed the man; and going to the bed, he gathered the two children into his arms, hushing and comforting them with soothing words. . . . .

"What on earth have you got there?" exclaimed Mrs. Wheaton as her husband came striding into the room where she sat mending one of his well-worn garments.

"Two babies!" he answered, in a voice so unusual that Mrs. Wheaton dropped her work on the floor and rose up in amazement.

"What?"

"Mrs. Grant's two babies. I've been over to the funeral, and I tell you, Jane, it wasn't in me to see those two little things carted off to the almshouse. There wasn't a woman to look after them, no, not one. Every soul sneaked off but Polly Jones, and she's of no account you know. Just look at their dear little faces!" And John Wheaton held them up in his arms, and let their tender, tearful, half-frightened, half-wondering eyes plead their own cause with his wife, and they did not plead in vain.

Surprised as she was, and with an instant's protest in her heart, Mrs. Wheaton could not, in the presence of these motherless little ones, utter a word of remonstrance.

She took the youngest one from the arms of her husband and spoke to it tenderly. The child sobbed two or three times, and then laid its head against her bosom.

There was an ocean of mother-love in the heart

of this woman, who had never been a mother, the instant her breast felt the pressure of the baby's head, and the arm that drew it closer with an involuntary impulse, was moved by this new love.

Not many words passed between the husband and wife—at least, not then—though thought was very busy with both of them.

Mrs. Wheaton's manner toward the children was kind even to tenderness; and this manner won their confidence and drew from them such little expressions of satisfaction as touched her heart and filled it with loving interest.

After nightfall when supper was over and the children asleep, Mr. and Mrs. Wheaton sat down together, each showing a little reserve and embarrassment. Mrs. Wheaton was the first to speak.

"What were you thinking about, John?" she said, almost sharply. "I can't have these children."

John Wheaton did not lift his eyes or reply, but there was a certain dogged and resolute air about him that his wife noticed as unusual.

"Somebody else must take them," she continued.

"The county?" replied her husband, testily.

"Yes. There's room for them at the almshouse, and no where else that I know of, unless they stay here.

"Unless they stay here," she repeated. Mrs. Wheaton's voice rose a little. "It's easy enough to say that, but who is to care for them?"

"It's a great undertaking, I know," answered

the husband, meekly, yet with a new quality in his voice that did not escape the quick ear of his wife, "and the burden must fall on you."

"I wouldn't mind that so much, but—"

She kept back the sentence that was on her tongue.

"But what?" asked her husband.

"John," said Mrs. Wheaton, drawing herself up in a resolute manner, and looking steadily in her husband's face, "as things are going on—"

"Things shall go on differently," interrupted Wheaton. "I've thought it all over."

"How differently, John?"

"Oh! in every way I'll turn over a new leaf."

John Wheaton saw a light flash into his wife's face.

"First and foremost, I'm not going to lose any more days. Last month I had six days docked from my wages."

"Why, John!"

"It's true—more's the shame for me. That was eighteen dollars, you see, not counting the money I fooled away with idle company—enough to pay for all these babies would eat and wear, twice over."

"Oh, John!" There was something eager and hopeful in his wife's face as she leaned toward him.

"I'm in downright earnest, Jane," he answered. "If you'll take the babies, I'll do my part. I'll turn over a new leaf. There shall be no more lost days; no more foolish wasting of money; no more spending of evenings at McBride's."

"Oh, John!" In her surprise and delight she could only repeat the exclamation. As she did so, she rose, and putting her hands on his shoulders, bend and kissed him on the forehead.

"You'll take the babies?" said he.

"Yes, and twenty more, if you keep to this, and stay so," answered Jane, laughing through her tears.

"OH, JOHN"

"All right, then, it's a bargain," and John Wheaton caught his wife's hand and shook it by way of confirmation.

From that time Mr. Wheaton turned over a new leaf. Neighbors expressed surprise when it was known that John and Jane Wheaton had adopted the two orphan children. Fellow workmen taunted John, calling him a soft-hearted fool, for "taking other men's brats."

One said to him, "Are four mouths easier to fill than two?" Another, "You'll be sick of this before the year's out." Another, "I'll see you sold out by the constable in less than six months."

But John had little to say in reply, only maintaining an air of quiet good humor and showing more interest in his work.

For three weeks John Wheaton had not lost a day — something very unusual; and not one evening during that time had he spent at McBride's saloon.

His poor little house, which had come to have a neglected look, was putting on a new appearance. The gate that for months had hobbled on one hinge, now swung smoothly, and the mended latch held it shut. Rank weeds no longer filled the dooryard. The broken steps were mended, and clean panes of glass filled many places in the sash where had been unsightly rags and sheets of paper.

Within, pleasant changes were also apparent. Various new but inexpensive pieces of furniture were to be found. Old things were mended, polished up, and wonderfully improved. With all of this, marvellous to relate, Wheaton's earnings had not only been equal to the increased expenditures, but there was an actual surplus of ten dollars in hand.

"I never would have believed it," said John, as he and his wife sat one evening talking over their improved condition, after the babies — loved now almost as if their own — were asleep.

"It's just as old Brown used to say, 'Waste takes more than want.' I declare I've got heart in me again. I thought we should have to let the place go; that I'd never be able to pay off the mortgage. But here we are, ten dollars ahead in less than a month; and going on at this rate, we'll have the home clear in about eighteen months.

"By the way, Jane, have you noticed how that pretty running rose, that we have trained over the doorway,— the one that used to look so forlorn and neglected,— is already beginning to push out its young leaves and buds? It's beautiful, isn't it? Oh, I'm so glad we shall be able to keep the old home!"

Beautifying the Home

Next day a fellow workman said to John Wheaton, half in banter, "Didn't I see the constable down your way yesterday?"

"I shouldn't wonder," replied Wheaton, with more gravity of manner than his questioner had expected.

"I thought I saw him looking around after things, and counting his fees on his fingers."

"Likely as not," replied Mr. Wheaton. "I know of a good many rents not paid up last quarter. Money gone to McBride's instead of the landlord —eh?"

The man winced a little.

"How are the babies?" he asked.

"First rate," Mr. Wheaton answered, with a smile so real that his fellow workman could not continue his banter.

Time went on, and to the surprise of all, John Wheaton's circumstances kept improving. The babies had brought a blessing to his home. In less than eighteen months, he had paid off the mortgage that for years had rested on his little home; and not only this, he had improved it in various ways, even to putting up a small addition, so as to give them a neat breakfast room.

The children grew finely,—there were three of them now,—for their hearts and home had opened to another orphan baby. The three little ones were carefully trained by Mrs. Wheaton, and had become the light and joy of the household.

————

Five years have passed away. John Wheaton is a master workman and employs ten men. He has enlarged his house, and made it one of the neatest in the village.

Among his men is the very one who bantered him the most about the children and prophesied

"I guess we'll have to take a baby or two."

that he would soon be sold out by the constable. Poor man! it was not long before the constable had him in charge. He had wasted his money at McBride's, instead of paying it to the landlord.

Walking home one evening after his work was done, John Wheaton and his journeyman took the same way. They were silent until they came near the former's pretty dwelling, when the journeyman said, half in jest, yet with undisguised bitterness, "I guess we'll have to take a baby or two."

"Why?"

"For good luck," the other one replied.

"Oh!"

"You've had nothing but good luck ever since you took Mrs. Grant's orphan children."

"Only such good luck as any one may have, if he will," answered Wheaton.

"I can't see it," returned the other somewhat bitterly. "Your wages were no better than mine. I had one child, and you saddled yourself with two, and not long afterward added a third. And how is it to-day? You have a nice house, and your wife and children are well dressed, while I have never been able to make ends meet, and my boy looks like a ragamuffin half the time."

"Do you see that house over there—the largest and handsomest in the place?" asked Wheaton.

"Yes."

"Who owns it?"

"Jimmy McBride."

"How much did you pay toward the building of it?"

"Me?" in surprise.

"Yes, you. How much did you pay toward the building of it?"

"Why, nothing. Why should I help pay for his house?"

"Sure enough! Why should your hard earnings go to build and furnish an elegant house for a man who would rather sell liquor, and so ruin his neighbors, body and soul, than support himself in a useful calling, as you and I are trying to do?"

"I can't see what you're driving at," replied his companion.

"How much do you spend at McBride's saloon every week?"

The man stood still with a blank look on his face.

"A dollar a week?" asked Mr. Wheaton.

"Yes."

"Say a dollar and a half?"

"Well, say as much."

"Do you know what that amounts to in a year?"

"Never counted it up."

"Seventy-eight dollars."

"No!"

"Yes, to a dollar. So, in five years, at this rate, you have contributed nearly four hundred dollars toward McBride's handsome house, without getting anything but harm in return, and haven't a shingle over your head that you can call your own.

"Now it's my advice, in a friendly way, that you stop helping McBride and begin to help yourself.

He's comfortable enough, and can do without your dollar and a half a week. Take a baby, for good luck, as you call it, if you will. You'll find one over at the poorhouse; it won't cost you half as much as helping McBride, and I don't think he needs your aid any longer. But here we are at home, and I see my wife and children waiting for me. Come in, won't you?"

"No, thank you. I'll go home and talk to Ellen about taking a baby for good luck."

And he tried to smile, as he called back, after a few steps:—

"If you see anything of my Jack about your place, just send him home, won't you?"

Jack was there, dirty, and meanly dressed, and in striking contrast with John Wheaton's three adopted children, who, with the only mother they knew, gave the happy man a joyful welcome.

"I have turned over a new leaf," said the journeyman when he came to work the next morning.

"Indeed! I am glad to hear it," returned Mr. Wheaton.

"Ellen and I talked it over last night. I am done helping saloon keepers build handsome houses. I'm glad you put it to me in that way. I never looked at it so before. But it's just the hard truth. What fools we are!"

"Going to take a baby?" questioned Mr. Wheaton, smiling.

"Well, we haven't just settled that; but Ellen heard yesterday of a poor little thing that would have to go to the county house unless some one agrees to take it, and I shouldn't wonder now if she opened her heart,—for she's a motherly body."

"Where is it?" asked Mr. Wheaton.

"Down at the Woodbury mills."

"Look here, Frank. Take my advice, and put this baby between you and McBride's saloon."

Only a little while did the man hesitate. Then he exclaimed:—

"I'll do it!"

"Do it at once, then," said Mr. Wheaton. "Put on your coat and go over to the mills and get the baby. It will be an angel in your house, that will help and bless you in every hour of temptation. Go at once. God has opened for you this way of safety, and if you walk therein, all will be well."

He did walk therein, and all *was* well. Mr. Wheaton's prophesy was fulfilled. In less than two years, the journeyman had his own roof over his head, and it covered a happy home.

IN THE HOUSE OF HIS FRIENDS

BY MRS. L. D. AVERY-STUTTLE

EA, mine own familiar friend, in whom I trusted, . . . hath lifted up his heel against me."

The largest church in Jonesville was well filled that Sabbath, for it was communion day, and the eloquent Mr. Barnes was to fill the pulpit, and officiate with the pastor at the Lord's table.

The congregation was very select,—in fact, it was mostly composed of the well-to-do residents of the town; and the Master's words, "The poor ye have always with you," would hardly have seemed an appropriate text—especially on this particular morning.

But there was one gentle little woman, with a child in her arms and a little girl by her side, who sat in a pew far up in front, toward the right of the altar, in whose dark eyes there lurked a shadow, and in whose heart had entered a terrible fear.

The man who sat beside her was a noble looking fellow, broad of shoulder, strong of limb, stalwart of frame. But to a close observer there still appeared marks of past dissipation and reckless intemperance, which had left there unmistakable tokens on cheek and brow,—tokens which even the

(127)

charitable hand of time must be many years in effacing altogether.

And it had been only one little year since Burton Holbrook had been plucked even as a brand from the burning; but in all the year, not once had the accursed cup touched his lips.

Burton Holbrook could not remember when he had first learned to love the cup; the terrible heritage had been his from birth,—a heritage bequeathed him by his poor father, whose drunken carousals had made his childhood miserable.

And so the heritage of thirst had been his; and he had fought it manfully, bravely all the years. But the record of the years had been filled with shameful defeat so often that the little woman by his side had been well nigh discouraged many times.

But in the past few months a new hope had been born,—a hope bright with anticipation and big with promise.

For Burton Holbrook had been converted and joined the church.

"You can never conquor in your own strength," she had said; and her prayers had ascended day and night unceasingly. And one glad day he had come to her, with a new light in his eyes and a new song upon his lips.

Then, almost as if by magic, prosperity seemed to come to them by leaps and bounds; friends multiplied; a position was offered him, lucrative beyond his wildest dreams. Within the year, the humble home had been exchanged for a pleasant cottage on one of the better streets, and from this cottage ascended night and morning, songs and prayers of thanksgiving and praise.

And this Sabbath he was attending communion service for the first time.

Strange that sad thoughts should intrude,—that unwelcome fears, and dim, shadowy forebodings should come trooping into the heart of the little woman by his side,—to-day of *all* days,—to-day, when her cup of joy was full to the brim!

"*Songs of thanksgiving and praise*"

In the very beginning of the services, she had suddenly remembered that it was communion day,— yes, yes, she had known that, all the time. But now she realized with a dull pain at her heart, that there would be wine. There must be; and it would be the wine that intoxicates!

Ah! too well she knew the demons that forever dogged her husband's footsteps! Given the slightest opportunity, and they were about him in troops.

9

Was there, then, no spot too sacred for them to invade? Was there to be no safety, even within the sacred courts of the house of the Lord?

In her perfect happiness, she had not given it a thought; but now, she wondered vaguely why she had not remembered. Ah, once before, in those awful days that seemed so long, long ago,—once before, a single taste of red wine had been his undoing!

How helpless she felt, as she sat by his side and glanced timidly up into his handsome face—her noble husband! And she reflected that she had urged him to unite with the church long before he had thought of offering himself. She had told him that this would be such a source of strength to him! And now she shuddered.

Why had no one cared for his soul? Why had no voice been raised in protest? And then she remembered hearing Mrs. Jones, the deaconess, once say that she had protested against this thing; but the pastor had only smiled and treated the matter lightly,—in fact he had gone so far as to insinuate that "it would be casting a reflection upon the respectability" of his eminently respectable congregation, to offer them new wine at communion, when they had always been accustomed to the old!

So it would have been of no use for her to protest. The pastor would have scorned her husband as a weakling—her strong, noble husband.

But see, the red wine has already been uncovered; the blessing has been pronounced,—ah, surely it is only the emblem of the spilled blood of the Man of Sorrows!

Burton Holbrook starts. His face is white as chiseled marble. His breath comes in quick, hard gasps. Already the subtle scent of the red wine is in his nostrils.

The little woman marks with strange distinctness, the white, delicate fingers of the pastor, as he offers the glass to her husband,—for they are in the pew near the altar. The words which the minister had read that morning, ring in her ears: "Yea, mine own familiar friend, in whom I trusted, . . . hath lifted up his heel against me."

She turns her eyes in sickening fear upon the man. His face is gray and drawn, the muscles of his neck are working, and the blue veins are standing out upon his forehead. He turns his eyes in piteous appeal toward his wife, then toward the pastor. Then over his haggard face there flits an expression of mad desire. The fiends of darkness are tapping upon his forehead and beckoning to him insistently.

Even the pastor starts with alarm as Burton Holbrook reaches his trembling fingers toward the glass. A fire like the smouldering fires of the pit leaps into his dark eyes,—and the glass is drained.

There was an uneasy, expectant rustle in the congregation. The minister turned his eyes for a moment. It was enough. Burton Holbrook sprang like a famished tiger and snatched at the pitcher. In a moment more, it was empty.

" Down the long aisle rushed a frenzied, hatless man"

(132)

Then, down the long aisle of horrified, frightened faces, and out into the quiet streets, rushed a frenzied, hatless man.

———

Over at the saloon on the nearest corner, lingered a few of the former companions of Burton Holbrook, discussing their old comrade, over their cups:—

"Been almost a year, I think, hasn't it, since Holbrook last favored us with his company?" questioned the bartender sneeringly, as he handed a foaming glass to a young man whose trembling hand and thick speech told a pitiful story of disease and dissipation.

"Considers himself mighty good, I reckon," was the reply.

"I've done everything I could to get him to give up those high and lofty notions of his," shamelessly admitted another.

"I'm right glad I don't have to sell *my* liberty," blustered Jack Hartwell, "and I told him so the other day; but he had an answer ready, of course. Real, reg'lar parson, Burt's got to be, since he's quit us."

"That makes me think," stammered an old man from across the room, "Holbrook's gone and joined the church, so they say,—got clear off the devil's ground, I s'pose he thinks, now,— but,—" and the old man lowered his voice, while a hateful grin distorted his bloated face, "but we'll see—we'll see. He's no whit better than the rest of us, that he should,—"

"No," interrupted the bartender, with an oath, "somebody's likely been preachin' to him. But if he thinks he's safe, just because —"

But the bartender never finished his speech. Into the midst of them rushed a man, breathless and hatless, with haggard face and wild, hollow eyes.

"Let me drink, man! let me drink! I've sold my soul for it. The demons of hell have got me this time! I have held my own against them for a year,—but they caught me,—caught me in the church,—and—and I *will die*, but I *must* have my drink!"

Within another month, delirium tremens, with its unspeakable horrors, had claimed its victim.

But I am glad to say that now there is *one* church in Jonesville, which offers nothing but pure, sweet, new wine at communion.

But still a poor, heartbroken little woman murmurs over and over again, "'Woe unto him that giveth his neighbor drink!'"

THE SIGN BOARD

EVERYBODY liked Tom Hall, and everybody was sorry for him. It was sad to see such a fine young man a victim of drunkenness, and Tom had fallen into the mocker's power unwittingly, it seems. A new saloon had been opened close to the foundry at which he worked, and he, along with others, was in the habit of going in for a glass of beer.

When the cold weather set in, he took something stronger, until he began to imagine that spirits agreed with him. Tom went on, and the liking for strong drink increased, until at all hours he might be seen staggering out of the "Rainbow," dizzy and stupefied with the intoxicating cup.

Tom's was a very sad case. He belonged to a respectable family, and he had been religiously trained, and until he was drawn into the snare, he was an affectionate son and brother. Friends counseled, and minister's preached, and every means was tried to reclaim him, but all effort seemed lost, — Tom was bound hard and fast with the invisible chains of the "mocker." His family mourned him as lost, and many a silent tear his sister dropped on his tattered garments as she sat darning and patching them.

"Ah, these rents will not darn again," said

Jennie, as she turned over Tom's ragged raiment. In Tom's better days, he had pride, and it was a sad change when he didn't care who saw him "out at the elbows."

But somehow Jennie could not find it in her heart to abandon the brother she still loved, and so Tom's tattered garments were taken up again, and made the most of.

"*Kindness* may win him back," said Jennie, and when he came home at the worst, he was met in peace,— if in sorrow.

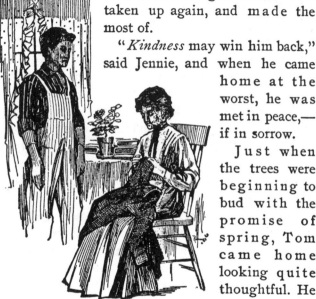

"*That's tiresome work, Jennie.*"

Just when the trees were beginning to bud with the promise of spring, Tom came home looking quite thoughtful. He was sober after a long run.

In the last rays of the setting sun, his sister was trying to cover some old darns.

Tom stood beside her, and silently watched the patient fingers for some time.

"That's tiresome work, Jennie," he said. His sister held up her seam before him.

"Why, that is a bunch of rags," said Tom.

"Yes, Tom ; and a bunch of rags would be the best sign board that a saloon keeper could hang over his door," said Jennie, sadly.

Tom made no reply. He looked at the rags in silence.

Next morning Tom went back to his work and continued steady for two or three weeks.

He looked toward the "Rainbow," but didn't go in.

"Hello! what's up with Tom Hall?" wondered Sinclair, as he filled up a glass of Tom's favorite whisky for another customer at the counter.

Sinclair was not the only one who was astonished at the change.

Every day Tom went to his work; every night he came home sober, and after a time he appeared at church on the Sabbath. Then people began to believe that Tom was in earnest, and really meant to reform.

"Has Tom Hall really become a teetotaler?" queried Sinclair, when a whole month had passed without a visit to the "Rainbow."

Well, it seemed so, for nothing stronger than water had passed his lips since that night on which his sister had shown him the bunch of rags. "I'll have a talk with Tom and learn how he got off the scent, though," Sinclair resolved.

An opportunity came sooner than he expected. In the beginning of summer a terrific thunderstorm passed over Airlie, and among the general devastation, Sinclair's sign board was shivered to atoms.

Tom happened to be passing the "Rainbow" next morning, and stopped to glance up at the old mark.

"Fine work here, the storm's done for us, remarked Mr. Sinclair, who was standing in his door, "and I'll have to get a new sign board."

"Is it so bad as that?" asked Tom.

"Yes, the 'Rainbow' is in shivers."

"Then you'll want a new sign board," suggested Tom.

"Of course; isn't that what I'm telling you?"

"Is it to be the 'Rainbow' again?" asked Tom.

"I suppose so," answered Mr. Sinclair, "unless you can give a new idea, Tom."

"I think I can," returned Tom; "but I must go home first."

"Don't forget, though," said Mr. Sinclair.

"But you're a stranger now-a-days, by the by, Tom."

"I won't be long," answered Tom, as he hurried toward home.

A better sign board than "The Rainbow" Mr. Sinclair did not expect to get; he was only joking with Tom Hall, and he raised his eyebrows when Tom made his appearance, with a bundle under his arm, and requested him to look at the new sign board.

"I didn't think you would catch me up; but step in, Tom, and let me see your idea."

Tom gravely undid his bundle, and held up a

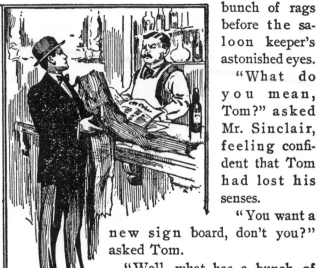

bunch of rags before the saloon keeper's astonished eyes.

"What do you mean, Tom?" asked Mr. Sinclair, feeling confident that Tom had lost his senses.

"You want a new sign board, don't you?" asked Tom.

"Well, what has a bunch of rags got to do with that?" said Mr. Sinclair.

"Ask yourself, sir, if a bunch of rags is not the best sign board that can hang across your door," said Tom, and his lips quivered.

"Was it that bunch of rags that made you a teetotaler, Tom?" said Mr. Sinclair, more confused than he liked to confess.

"It was one of the means, sir," answered Tom, "and, perhaps some poor wretch, seeing in this bunch of rags the future outcome of drink, will bless you for the sign board."

Tom walked away to his work, and Mr. Sinclair went back to his counter, but all day the bunch of rags troubled him.

It was a busy day, but every new comer seemed more deplorably wretched and worse off than the last served.   He was thankful when night came.

The last customer was a woman literally covered with rags.   A little infant sat on her arm.   It was crying with cold and hunger.

"Go home and put clothes on your child," said Mr. Sinclair, flinging back the money the woman had laid down.

"I have nothing but rags," said the woman.

"Tom is right," said Mr. Sinclair; "the end of drink is misery and rags, and the man who has a taste for that sort of thing may put his name on the *new sign board*."

DAN NAYLOR'S LEGACY

WHEN Enoch Wilton died, people said that Daniel Naylor was sure to come into possession of a handsome property, since his Uncle Enoch was known to be a man of some means, and Daniel was his favorite nephew.

But when the will was read, they changed their minds, for the only clause it contained which referred to Daniel read as follows:—

"And to Daniel Naylor, my beloved nephew, I give and bequeath the framed copy of the temperance pledge to which, under Divine Providence, I owe salvation from a drunkard's grave; also to this I owe all the material prosperity which has gladdened my latter years. And I recommend that he remove it from its frame, and affix his signature beneath mine; satisfied that he will find the pledge an unfailing source of wealth to him, as it has been to me."

Daniel Naylor resented this, as he was a drinking man, and he indignantly stowed away his uncle's bequest, among the rubbish in the attic, assuring his wife that, as his uncle had treated him so shabbily, he should not trouble himself further about it; and there, for years, it slumbered, utterly forgotten.

Meanwhile, Daniel Naylor's affairs went from bad to worse, for his drinking habits had strengthened their hold upon him.

One day, about five years after his uncle's death, he returned to his now squalid home, to tell his wife that the last cent had gone, and that "Squire Grip," the village lawyer, would, the next day, fore-close the mortgage on their little place, leaving them homeless.

"Oh Daniel!" exclaimed the poor woman in a tone of despair, "What shall we do? Where can we go?"

"I do not know," he responded moodily,—"to the poorhouse, perhaps."

"Don't say that, Daniel!" pleaded the wife, "you still have two hands left, and if—"

"I cannot get employment," he interrupted. "I have been to all my employers and to all my friends; I can assure you that I have made every effort possi-ble. But somehow, they don't act toward me as they used to, in the old days when I was more pros-perous. I don't know what's the matter, I'm sure. They only shake their heads and say they are sorry, but the times are so hard they cannot give me work. I shall have to give it up."

"But you must not give it up, there must be employment somewhere."

"But I tell you, I am unable to find it. I have tried everywhere; there is nothing for me to do."

"Look here, Dainel, if you will promise me just one thing, I'll tell you how you can find work,— Oh, if you would only promise, Daniel!" and Mrs. Naylor glanced appealingly at her husband.

Daniel Naylor felt a trifle uncomfortable, for he

saw traces of tears in his wife's eyes, and she had rarely spoken to him so earnestly. But he only stammered brokenly :—

"What are the conditions?"

"Will you promise?"

"I would rather know the conditions first."

"The conditions are that you quit your drinking habits and sign the temperance pledge."

Daniel Naylor started.

"What!" he cried, in astonishment. "Do you intend to say that my drinking a little, now and then, interferes with my getting work to do?"

"It certainly does, Daniel," was the sorrowful reply, "for I have heard at least one of your old employers say as much."

"Who was it?"

"Mr. Field."

"What did he say?"

"You recollect the time, about three weeks ago, when you were— were—"

"Drunk."

"Yes, when you were drunk. You were at work for him then, and when he came after you, and I told him you could not come, he guessed the truth, and I heard him say to his clerk, who was with him, as he drove off :—

"'Well, this is the second time Dan Naylor has failed me when I needed him most, but I shall be sure he does not do it again.'

"And that, my husband, is the source of almost all our trouble, as I believe you, yourself, will admit when you think the matter over; you can't imagine how it makes me feel." And Mrs. Naylor put her apron to her eyes and sobbed hysterically.

It was Daniel Naylor's turn to reflect now,—and it was not the first time, by any means. This subject had long been troubling him. But it was very hard for him to acknowledge or to realize that his deep poverty and misery had been brought about by his own conduct.

"Well, I believe you are right," he said, at last. "But what can I do? Our home is gone, and I have lost the confidence of my employers,

"Seven one thousand dollar notes fell out."

—so signing the pledge cannot amount to much."

"Yes, it would amount to a great deal. It would restore your self-respect, and in a great measure you would be able to regain their confidence."

Then came another period of silence. At last a great purpose entered his heart, and the light of a firm resolve shone in his eyes.

"Bring me a paper, and I *will sign it*, and may God give me strength to keep it!"

"Why not sign Uncle Enoch's pledge?" his wife inquired. "I saw it lying up in the attic the other day, and if you wish, I will bring it."

"Certainly; that will save writing another."

The pledge was soon brought, and Daniel Naylor removed it from the frame and placed it on the table. As he did so, a roll of brown paper fell out of its back and dropped unnoticed at his feet.

After he had signed his name under that of his uncle, he turned to replace the pledge in its frame.

In doing this, his eyes fell upon the small roll of brown paper lying on the floor.

Stooping to pick it up, he uttered a sudden cry of astonishment, as he saw the corner of a bank note protruding; with trembling fingers, he undid the package, to find *seven one thousand dollar notes*, and a scrap of paper on which was written:—

"Is not the pledge a sure road to wealth?"

"God bless good Uncle Enoch!" he exclaimed fervently. I can now take up the mortgage, and as for the pledge, I will keep that sacred as long as I live."

And his wife responded with a fervent—

"Amen."

10

"DON'T LET HIM HAVE IT"

IF they wouldn't let him have it!" exclaimed Mrs. Leslie, weeping; "Oh! if they wouldn't sell him the liquor, there'd not be any trouble. He's one of the best of men when he does not drink. He does not bring liquor into the house; and he tries very hard, I know, to keep sober, but he cannot pass Jenk's tavern."

Mrs. Leslie was talking with a sympathizing neighbor, who responded by saying, "It's a downright shame!"

While this conversation was going on, a little girl, of about six years, sat listening attentively. After a little while she went quietly from the room, and took her way down the road unobserved by the mother.

There was a purpose, great and noble, in her mind; she had started on a mission. "Oh, if they wouldn't sell him liquor!" Those earnest words of her mother filled her thoughts. If Mr. Jenks wouldn't sell her father drink, there would be no more trouble. How simple the remedy!

She would go to Mr. Jenks and ask him not to let her father have any more liquor, and all would be well again. Artless, innocent child!

The tavern kept by Jenks — the laziest man in Milanville, stood nearly a quarter of a mile from the tenement occupied by the Leslies. Toward this place, under a hot sun, Lizzie made her way, her mind so filled with its purpose, that she was unconscious of heat or fatigue.

Not long before, a traveler had alighted at the tavern door. After giving directions to have his horse fed, he entered the barroom, where Jenks stood behind the counter.

"Have something to drink?" inquired the landlord.

"I'll take a glass of water, if you please."

Jenks could not hide the indifference at once felt toward the stranger. Very deliberately he set a pitcher and glass upon the counter, and then turned partly away. The stranger poured out a full tumbler of water, and drank it with an air of satisfaction.

"Good water, that of yours, landlord," said he.

"Is it?" was returned somewhat uncourteously.

"I call it good water, don't you?"

"Never drink water by itself." As Jenks said this, he winked to one of his customers, who was lounging on the bar. "In fact, it's so long since I drank any water that I forget how it tastes. Don't you, Leslie?"

The man to whom this was addressed was not so far lost to shame as Jenks. He blushed and looked confused as he replied :—

"It might be better for some of us if we had not lost our relish for water."

"A true word spoken, my friend!" said the stranger, turning to the man, whose swollen visage, and patched, threadbare garments, too plainly told the story of his life.

"Water, pure water, bright water! is my motto. Its attendants are health, thrift, and happiness. It takes not away the child's bread, nor the toiling wife's garments."

There were two or three customers at the bar besides Leslie, to whom this was addressed; and all of them, in spite of the landlord's angry and sneering countenance, treated the stranger with attention and respect. Seeing this, Jenks could not restrain himself; so, advancing to the gentleman's side, and laying his hand rudely on his shoulder, he said in a peremptory manner:—

"See here, my friend, if you are about to deliver a temperance lecture, you can adjourn to the town hall or the Methodist chapel."

The stranger moved aside a pace or two, and then said, mildly, "there must be something wrong here, if a man may not speak in praise of water without giving offense."

"I said you could adjourn your lecture." The landlord's face was now a fiery red, and he spoke with insolence and passion.

"Oh, well, as you are president of the meeting, I suppose we must let you exercise an arbitrary power of judgment," said the stranger; "I didn't think any one had so strong a dislike of water as to consider its praise an insult."

At this moment a child stepped into the barroom. She glanced neither to the right nor the left, but walked up to the landlord, lifted her sweet young face, and said in tones that thrilled every heart but his, "Please, Mr. Jenks, don't sell papa any more liquor!"

"Off home with you, this instant!" exclaimed

"Please, Mr. Jenks, don't sell papa any more liquor."

Jenks. As he spoke, he advanced toward the child with his uplifted hand in a threatening attitude.

"Please don't, Mr. Jenks," persisted the child, not moving or taking her eyes from the landlord's countenance. "Mother says if you would not sell him liquor, there'd be no trouble. He's kind and good to us all when he does not drink."

"Off, I say!" shouted Jenks, now maddened beyond self-control, and his hand was about to descend upon the little one, when the stranger caught her in his arms, exclaiming as he did so, with deep emotion:—

"God bless the child! No! no, precious one," he added, "Don't fear him. Plead for your father. Plead for your home. Your petition must prevail. The merciful Lord cannot say nay to the little ones, whose angels do always behold the face of their Father in Heaven. God bless the child!" added the stranger, in a choking voice. "Oh, that the father, for whom she has come on this touching errand, were present now! If there was anything of manhood yet left in him, this would awaken it from its palsied sleep."

"Papa! O papa!" the child exclaimed, stretching forth her hand. In the next moment she was clinging to the breast of her father, who, with his arms clasped tightly around her, stood weeping and mingling his tears with those of his child.

An oppressive stillness reigned in the room! Jenks stood subdued and bewildered, his state of mental confusion scarcely enabling him to comprehend the full import of the scene, and the stranger looked on wonderingly, yet deeply affected.

Quietly, and with moist eyes, the two or three customers, who had been lounging at the bar, went stealthily out; and the landlord, the stranger, and the father and the child, were left the only inmates of the room.

"Come, Lizzie, dear! this is no place for us," said Leslie, breaking the dead silence. "We'll go home." And the unhappy father took his child by the hand, and led her toward the door.

But the little one held back. "Wait, papa,

wait," she said : "he hasn't promised, yet. Oh, I
wish he would promise!"

"Promise her, in heaven's name!" exclaimed the
stranger.

"If I do promise,
I keep it!" returned
the landlord, in a
threatening tone.

"Then, in the
name of mercy, do
promise, begged Les-
lie, in a despairing
voice: "promise, and
I'm safe!"

"Be it so! May I
be cursed, if ever I
sell you a drop of
drink at this bar,
while I am land-
lord!" Jenks spoke
with an angry em-
phasis.

"God be thanked!" murmured the poor drunkard, as he led his child away. "God be thanked!
There is hope for me yet."

Hardly had Mrs. Leslie missed her child ere she
entered, leading her father by the hand. "O mother!" she exclaimed, with a joy-lit countanence and
a voice of exultation, "Mr. Jenks has promised!"

"Promised what?" Hope sprang up in the
mother's heart; her face flushed, then grew pale.

"That he would never sell me another glass of liquor," replied the husband.

A pair of thin, white hands were clasped together; an ashen face was turned upward; tearful eyes looked their thankfulness in Heaven.

"There is hope yet," said Leslie.

"Hope, hope! And, O Edward, you have said the word. I know you will be a man once more now! Surely, God sent our child on that errand of love! Innocence has triumphed over vice and cruelty. Our child came to the strong, evil, passionate man, and in her weakness and innocence, prevailed over him. God made her fearless and eloquent."

A year afterward, a stranger came that way, and stopped at the same old tavern. As before, Jenks was behind his well-filled bar, and drinking customers came and went in numbers.

Jenks did not recognize the stranger until he called for water, and drank a full tumbler of the pure liquid with a hearty zest. Then he knew him, but feigned to be ignorant of his identity.

The stranger made no reference to the scene he had witnessed twelve months before, but lingered in the barroom most of the day, closely observing every one who came there to drink. Leslie was not among the number.

"What has become of the man and the little girl that I saw here at my last visit to Milanville?" the stranger questioned.

"Gone to the devil, for all I care," was the landlord's rude answer as he hastily left the barroom.

"Do you see that little white cottage away off there, just at the edge of the wood?" replied one of the customers. "A row of tall poplars stand in front. The young man you ask for lives there. And what is more, if he keeps on the way he has begun, the cottage will be his own in another year."

"Ah! I see; well, did the young man Leslie ever again try to get a drink here, since the landlord promised never to let him have another?"

"Twice to my knowledge."

"And he refused him?"

"Yes; if you remember, Jenks said, in his anger, 'May I be cursed if I sell him another drop.' That saved Leslie. Jenks is superstitious in some things. Once he drove Leslie from the barroom, threatening, at the same time, to horsewhip him if he ever set foot inside his house again."

"Ah! sometimes God makes even the wrath of man to praise Him," replied the stranger reverently.

ONLY THE HUSK

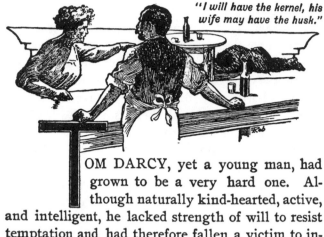

"I will have the kernel, his wife may have the husk."

TOM DARCY, yet a young man, had grown to be a very hard one. Although naturally kind-hearted, active, and intelligent, he lacked strength of will to resist temptation and had therefore fallen a victim to intemperance.

He had lost his position as foreman of a great machine shop, and what money he now earned came from odd jobs of tinkering which he was able to do at private houses here and there; for Tom was a genius as well as a mechanic, and when his head was steady enough, he could mend a clock or clean a watch, as well as he could set up and regulate a steam engine, and this latter he could do better than any man ever employed by the Scott Falls Manufacturing Company.

One day Tom was engaged to mend a broken mowing machine and reaper, for which he received five dollars; and, on the following morning, he started for his old haunt, the village tavern. He

(154)

knew that his wife sadly needed the money, and that his two little children were absolutely suffering for want of clothing; so that morning he held a debate with his better nature, but his better nature had become weak, and the demon of appetite carried the day.

So, away to the tavern Tom went, where, for two or three hours he felt the exhilarating effect of the strong drink and fancied himself happy because he could laugh and sing. He drank while he could stand, then lay down in a corner where his companions left him.

It was almost midnight, when the landlord's wife came to the barroom to see what kept her husband up, and she quickly saw Tom.

"Peter," said she, "why don't you send that miserable Tom Darcy home? He's been hanging around here long enough."

Tom's stupefaction was not sound sleep. The dead coma had left his brain, and the calling of his name stung his senses to keen attention. He had an insane love for rum, but he did not love the landlord.

Long years ago, Peter Tinder and Tom Darcy had wooed the same maiden,—Ellen Goss,—and Tom had won her, leaving Peter to take up with the sharp-tempered damsel who had brought him the tavern. Tom knew well enough that even lately Peter Tinder had gloated over the misery of the woman who had once discarded him.

"Why don't you send him home?" demanded

Mrs. Tinder, with an impatient stamp of her foot.

"Hush, Betsey, he's got money. Let him be, and he'll be sure to spend it before he goes home. I'll have the kernel of that nut and his wife may have the husk."

Betsey turned away, and shortly afterward Tom Darcy lifted himself upon his elbow.

"Ah, Tom, are you awake?"

"Yes."

"Then rouse up and have a warm glass."

Tom got upon his feet and steadied himself.

"No, I won't drink any more to-night."

"It won't hurt you, Tom,—just one glass."

"I know it won't!" said Tom, buttoning up his coat by the solitary button left. "I know it won't."

The air was damp and cold, but Tom Darcy didn't mind it. The fact was, he was waking up at last. The words of Peter Tinder were sounding in his ears. He would go home at once. Why had he not gone before? he wondered, as he stepped out into the dimly lighted street.

Tom stopped a moment and looked up at the stars and then looked down upon the earth.

"Ay," he muttered, grinding his heel into the gravel, "Peter Tinder is taking the kernel, and leaving poor Ellen the worthless husk,—a husk more than worthless. I am robbing my wife of joy; robbing my poor children of honor and comfort, and robbing myself of love and life, so that Peter Tinder may have the kernel and Ellen the husk. We'll see!"

It was a revelation to the man. The saloon-keeper's speech, meant not for his ears, had fallen upon his senses as fell the voice of the Risen One upon the ears of Saul of Tarsus.

"We'll see!"

"We'll see!" he repeated, setting his foot firmly upon the ground; and then he wended his way homeward.

On the following morning he said to his wife, "Ellen, have you any coffee in the house?"

"Yes, Tom." She did not tell him that her sister had given it to her. She was glad to hear him ask for coffee, instead of the old, old cider.

"I wish you would make me a cup, good and strong."

There was really music in Tom's voice, and his wife set about her work with a strange flutter at her heart.

Tom ate a light breakfast,—there was not much

left to eat in the house,—and then went out, with a resolute step, and walked straight to the great manufactory, where he found Mr. Scott in his office.

"Mr. Scott, I want to learn my trade over again."

"Eh, Tom, what do you mean?"

"I mean that it's Tom Darcy come back to the old place, asking forgiveness for the past, and hoping to do better in the future."

"Tom," cried the manufacturer, starting forward and grasping his hand, "are you in earnest? Is it really the old Tom?"

"It's what's left of him, sir, and we'll have him whole and strong very soon, if you'll only set him to work."

"Work! Ay, Tom, and bless you, too. There is an engine to be set up and tested to-day. Come with me."

Tom's hands were weak and unsteady, but his brain was clear, and under his skillful supervision the engine was set up and tested; but it was not perfect. There were mistakes which he had to correct, and it was late in the evening when the work was complete.

"How is it now, Tom?" asked Mr. Scott, as he came into the testing house and found the workmen ready to go home.

"She's all right now, sir. You may give your warrant without fear."

"God bless you, Tom! You don't know how like music the old voice sounds. Will you take your old place again?"

"Wait till Monday morning, sir. If you will offer it to me then, I will take it."

At the little cottage, Ellen Darcy's fluttering heart was sinking. That morning, after Tom had gone, she had found a dollar bill in the coffee cup.

"*I kept you waiting, Nellie*"

She knew that he had left it for her. She had been out and bought potatoes and sugar and flour and butter and a little basket of strawberries. All day long a ray of light had been dancing and glimmering before her, —a ray from the blessed light of other days. With prayer and hope she had set the tea-table and waited; but the sun went down and no Tom came. Eight o'clock, and almost nine.

Hark? The old step! quick, strong, eager, yes, it was Tom, with the old grime upon his hands and the odor of oil upon his clothing.

"I have kept you waiting, Nellie."

"Tom!"

"I did not mean to, but the work hung on."

"Tom! Tom!   You have been to the old shop!"

"Yes, and I'm promised the old place, and—"

"Oh, Tom!"

And she threw her arms around his neck and pressed a kiss upon his lips.

"Nellie, darling, wait a little, and you shall have the old Tom back again!"

"Oh, I have him now! God bless you, my husband!"

It was a banquet—that supper—with the bright angels of peace and love and joy spreading their wings over the board.

On the following Monday morning, Tom Darcy resumed his place at the head of the great machine shop, and those who thoroughly knew him had no fear of his going back into the slough of dissipation.

A few days later, Tom met Peter Tinder on the street.

"Eh, Tom, old boy, what's up?"

"*I'm* up,—right side up!"

"Yes, I see; but I hope you haven't forsaken us, Tom!"

"I have forsaken only the evil, Peter.   The fact is, I concluded that my wife and little ones had fed on 'husks' long enough, and if there was any goodness left in my heart or in my manhood, it was high time they had the benefit."

"Ah! you heard what I said to my wife that night."

"Yes, Peter, and I shall be grateful to you as long as I live. My remembrance of you will always be relieved by that tinge of brightness."

———

Ten years passed away. Peter Tinder had removed to a distant state. Long ago people had ceased declaring that Tom Darcy "would be as drunk as a fiddler before long."

The little cottage had been exchanged for a larger and more commodious home on one of the pleasantest streets. The two children, Paul and Emily, were growing to be a great help and comfort to their parents.

But you will want to know what became of Peter Tinder, the saloon keeper, into whose tills a large share of Tom Darcy's hard-earned money had found its way in the old days.

One bitter cold evening in mid-winter, the Darcy family sat around their cozy fireside. Suddenly the door bell rang. Gentle Mrs. Darcy, grown more sympathetic and charitable with the passing of the years, hurried to open the door. But she stepped back with a look of mingled pity and terror in her eyes.

There stood the most wretched creature she had ever seen. Trembling with the cold and covered with rags, he undertook to make known his errand :—

"Is this the home of Tom Darcy?"

By this time Tom was on his feet. "Come in, come in, man, don't stand out there, when there's

11

warmth inside; come right in, my poor fellow."

"I don't suppose you know me, Tom Darcy, or perhaps you wouldn't be so cordial," shivered the stranger, turning his bleared eyes toward his host.

There was something in the voice, which made Tom Darcy start:—

"Why, Ellen, wife, it's Pete,—Mr. Tinder! Why, man, where did you come from? What has happened?"

"Ah, it's many a year since anyone has called me *Mr.* Tinder,—'Old Pete'—that's the name I answer to *now-a-days.* I don't live anywhere,—I just wander till I find someone that'll take me in for the night."

While Ellen Darcy prepared a cup of hot milk and a large sandwich, "Old Pete" continued:—

"I heard you lived here, and that you were a Christian, Tom, and I reckoned you'd not turn me out to-night, though I never did you anything but evil,—I took the 'kernel' and you kept the 'husk' a long time, but things have turned about now. My wife died directly after we had left the old place, and then people began to say that "Old Pete" was his own best customer.

"I drank and drank until everything was gone. I often thought about the 'husk' and the 'kernel,' but I *must have the drink, Tom,* as long as I live, and that won't be long, please God."

Tom Darcy and his good wife made the poor wretch as comfortable as possible for the night, and entreated him to reform. But it was too late.

"Old Pete" had fed upon "husks" too long. Like
the prisoner of Chillon he had learned to love the
very chains which bound him.

As the wretched man started off toward the nearest saloon in the village, Tom Darcy watched him
with a strange fascination until the fluttering rags
had passed around the corner.

"But for the grace of God, Ellen," he said,
humbly, "I would be in his condition to-day, while
you and the children—"

Tom shuddered, while Ellen quoted tearfully :—

"'No drunkard shall inherit the kingdom of
God.'"

THE SERPENT IN THE HOME

IN all the town there was no brighter or more attractive girl than Miss Martin. Her elder sister had married one of the doctors of the place, and she came on a visit to her, and as was right and fitting, they enjoyed themselves by visiting places of interest together.

One day, while visiting a neighboring city, they stepped into a fashionable restaurant to rest and take refreshments. As it was a hot day, the sandwich was followed, at Dr. Black's suggestion, by a glass of wine.

Chemists tell us of the affinity of certain substances.

Dr. and Mrs. Black drank their glass of wine without any apparent effect. But it was different with Miss Martin. She had never drunk a whole glass of wine in all her life, and something in her system, I know not what or how, answered to its subtle qualities, and she felt its exhilarating effect. A pleasing, indescribable sensation came over her. Before, she was worn out and exhausted; now she felt light, vigorous, and happy. It is to constitutions of this kind, that stimulants are an unspeakable temptation.

Favoring circumstances, I grieve to say, were not wanting. Mrs. Black's callers were numerous, and wine and cake were regularly presented. They were asked to dinner and supper parties to get acquainted in the neighborhood, and at most of these parties wine was served, and just because other people took it, Miss Martin did so too.

She thought the place delightful and the people exceedingly pleasant; and if, in a forenoon, she felt exhausted and nervous after an evening's party, a glass of wine put her all right.

No wonder that, when she returned to her home, life seemed dull, flat, and heavy. She used to awake in the morning with a bright, cheery feeling, and begin to lay out her plan of work for the day. But things of an ordinary kind had no in-

The Doctor's Prescription

terest for her now. She became restless, her appetite failed, and she grew pale and thin.

Her mother, anxious and alarmed, called in the doctor, whose verdict was, "A little out of sorts — trying season of the year — liver dull — a little stimulant will set all to rights." Her father, good, confiding man, at once ordered in a dozen bottles of port wine, which was to be administered to the patient twice a day.

And so the flame was fanned and cherished, which in due time, — but I must not anticipate.

As I have said, Miss Martin was a very prepossessing girl, admired by many; so in a little while, when on a second visit to her sister, no one was surprised when it was announced that she was to be married to one who stood high in the opinion of all, and who was, indeed, a young man of great worth and excellence.

It happened that winter that a Young Men's Mutual Improvement Society, a Scientific Association, and a Total Abstinence Society were organized in the town.

Now, into the first two of these, Dr. Black and Mr. Bennet, his intended brother-in-law, entered readily, and were quite willing to attend meetings, give readings, and deliver lectures; but as for a temperance society, — really, they saw no need.

"It seems almost an insult to introduce such a society among respectable people. No doubt there are many who should not drink because they cannot stop in time, and in such cases drink is a great

curse; but with us, it is different." And when
Mr. Bennet saw Miss Martin sipping her glass of
wine, he thought as of everything else about her,
how graceful it seemed, and how well the action
became her.   It was but a few months after their
marriage that the poor illusion was dispelled.

One day some friends of Mr. Bennet's had come
to make them a visit, and a few neighbors had been
asked to meet them at dinner.

The little entertainment was a great success.
Finally Mrs. Bennet left her guests in the dining
room, over their wine; she had intended to be gone
but a moment; but when seated by herself, with
the excitement over, a feeling of excessive fatigue
and languor came upon her.   As on other occa-
sions, she at once thought of a glass of wine.   This
was just the very time it was needed!   So without
further consideration, she drank one glass after

another, till before she knew it, she was sleeping
the sleep of a drunkard in her own elegant drawing room.

By-and-by the door was thrown open, and Mr.
Bennet, in his usual cheery voice, said, "Here we
are, Mary, all ready for your nice cup of coffee."

But, alas! there was no answering greeting, nothing but an inarticulate sound from the prostrate form on the rug. The company took in the situation but too well, and all retired as gracefully as possible, "sorry to see Mrs. Bennet so poorly," etc.

Mr. Bennet was bewildered. Of all the possibilities in life, this was the last that could have occurred to him; and there he sat, with that terrible, mysterious smile upon his face, which you may have seen on the face of a strong man when shame and agony were gnawing at his heart.

It would be tedious to record Mrs. Bennet's resolutions of amendment made and broken, to be again renewed with the same result. Her husband's patience was often abused, but still he was always so ready to forgive.

But the most long-suffering patience may be worn out at last, and it seemed to Mr. Bennet that the only chance was to send his wife — once his pride, as well as his joy — to one of those asylums for the drunkard, called "refuges." The arrangements were made, and the day on which she was to go appointed.

I shall never forget that afternoon. The poor husband was utterly prostrated by grief and shame by an outbreak of his wife the day before, and, as an old friend, he requested me to accompany her, for he could not trust himself, and feared his resolution would give way at the parting scene.

She, poor creature, not only acquiesced in the

plan, but earnestly besought her husband on her kness to help her to get free from the wretched slavery in which she lived. It is easy for people outside to speak, but I do think that the wretched slave to strong drink is to be pitied.

Poor Mrs. Bennet had been for some months  in this establishment, when her husband, hoping against hope, removed to the city of which I have spoken, with a view of giving her new scenes and new surroundings in her future life, and brought her home. How he congratulated himself; how his love and long-slumbering reverence revived, as week after week passed, and still she stood the trial!

"At evening time it shall be light."

Some time after this I was invited to the marriage of their only daughter. She was one of whom any mother might have been proud, and on whom her father doted.

I had been greatly gratified at hearing of my friend's continued reformation. When I arrived that summer evening, I found the three sitting together on the lawn under a spreading tree, enjoying the sweetest hour of all the day. The outward scene seemed a fitting symbol of the inward peace, and I caught myself whispering, "At evening time it shall be light."

Looking back on the past, it seemed as if we had awakened from a fearful nightmare, and were being reassured by the calm and peace of returning morning.

Next day, as the wedding guests were strolling through the grounds after the marriage, till lunch was announced, and everything seemed the embodiment of calmness and comfort, he would have been thought a hard-hearted prophet of evil who would have predicted the events of the following hours.

I stepped aside and went into the house to see if I could be of any assistance in the finishing of the arrangements. On looking into the dining room, what was my amazement to find the table furnished with a profusion of wines and brandies!

Thinking there must have been some strange mistake, I hurried out and sought Mr. Bennet, to whom I told what I had seen, suggesting that his orders must surely have been misunderstood.

For a moment, a look of surprise came into his face. "Not at all," said he; "you do not suppose I could let such an occasion as this pass without giving it all the honors?"

"Honors!"

I thought some people had strange ideas about honors. I implored him to alter his arrangements even yet. "Thanks," said he, "for your kind interest; but pray don't trouble yourself, you will see that all will go off well." And then, in a lower tone, "Mary has promised me."

With a sorrowful heart, I turned away. The party had not been long in the dining room, when I saw Mrs. Bennet, who had hitherto been acting the part of hostess with all the ease and grace, which in her early days had charmed so many, become suddenly pale, and seemed to be putting a strong restraint upon herself. I felt deeply grieved when I saw those around her carelessly sipping their wine, ignorant of the fierce war they were kindling within her.

At last she could restrain herself no longer; it seemed as if a thunderbolt had fallen among us, when suddenly she rose, and seizing a bottle, darted to the door.

Mr. Bennet's face turned ashy pale, and when he attempted to rise, his knees smote against each other, like the monarch of old when the handwriting on the wall announced his doom. When I got outside the door, the poor woman looked round on me with a half-triumphant, half-scared expression, and the brandy bottle was lying empty beside her.

I helped her to the bed, and the doctor was sent for; but no human power could save her. As we watched her tossing to and fro, wildly appealing for protection from the fiery serpents which she averred were swarming around her, I wondered if her husband did not ask himself if he had fulfilled that vow made long ago, of loving, cherishing, and *protecting* her, when he exposed her to that which was indeed the supremest danger possible,—the very smell of what, to her, was deadly poison.

At length the storm subsided; she lay wan and worn on her pillow. Leaning over her, I heard in a low whisper the words, "*they shall thirst no more.*" The pathos was inexpressible. These were her last words. No doubt there is pardon for the penitent drunkard as well as for the penitent thief,

"They shall thirst no more"

even at the eleventh hour; but turning away from that deathbed, I could but say, "Let me die the death of the righteous, and let my last end be like his."

I have spoken of some of the outward incidents of Mrs. Bennet's history, but who shall imagine her inner life? I am sure that the most exquisite tortures ever invented, fell very far short of those endured by this poor woman.

When bidding good-by to the silent and mournful mansion, where all had but the other day seemed so bright and happy, I felt with new emphasis the force of the wise man's words, "Look not thou upon the wine when it is red, when it giveth his color in the cup, when it moveth itself aright. At last it biteth like a serpent, and stingeth like an adder."

Let us turn to the stern lesson woven all through the warp and woof of the foregoing story,—of a young life ruined and a home broken up as the result of the social wineglass. Social custom and "treating" are responsible for more drunkards' graves than many are willing to acknowledge.

But who will speak for the brewer and distiller who institute open "missionary" campaigns to teach the children to drink that they may fill the breaks in the ranks caused by the passing of the old inebriates? God says to such :—

"Woe unto him that giveth his neighbor drink, that putteth the bottle to him, and maketh him drunken also."

WORK DONE INSIDE

ONE of my friends is a very earnest, shrewd man, who seems to know how to do the best thing at the right time. One day he was passing a gin shop in Manchester, England, when he saw a drunken man lying on the ground. The poor fellow had evidently been turned out of doors when all his money was gone. In a moment my friend hastened across the street, and entering a grocer's shop, asked the clerk : —

"Will you oblige me with the largest sheet of paper you have?"

"What for, my friend? What's the matter?"

"Oh! you shall see in a moment or two. Please get me the largest sheet you have."

The sheet of paper was soon brought.

"Now, will you lend me a piece of chalk?"

My friend then quickly printed, in large letters, these words : — "*SPECIMEN OF THE WORK DONE INSIDE.*"

He then fastened the paper onto the drunken man, and retired a short distance. In a few moments several passers-by stopped to read the notice, and in a short time a crowd assembled; then the saloon keeper, hearing the noise and laughter outside, came out to see what it was about. He eagerly

(174)

bent down and read the inscription on the paper, and then demanded in an angry voice : —

"Who did that?"

"Which?" asked my friend, who now joined the crowd. "If you mean what is written on the paper, I DID THAT; but if you mean the man, YOU DID THAT! This morning when he arose, he was sober; when he walked down the street, on his way to work, he was sober; when he went into your shop, he was sober; and now he is what you made him. Is he not a true specimen of the work done inside?"

NAT RAYMOND'S VICTORY AND WHAT CAME OF IT

OH, but I'll have the jolliest time, though! I'm going out to Uncle Nathan's, Christmas!" and Nat Raymond threw his cap high in the air. "Uncle Nathan's just splendid; I was named after him, wasn't I mother?"

Nat was too excited and delighted to wait for his mother to reply, and he continued:—

"I'm going to be a sailor, too, some day, mother, just like Uncle Nathan. I shall ask him to tell me all about the time when his ship got frozen in, up among the funny Esquimaux. And besides, I want him to tell me about those great big, furry dogs that used to draw him over the snow.

"Uncle Nathan's a great man,— don't you think so, mother? and of course he's just the *best* man!"

Nat paused at last, not so much because he really cared for his mother to answer him, but the fact was, he was quite out of breath.

"Yes, dear, your uncle is a kind-hearted man, but I am so sorry to say, he has *one* bad habit.

I've tried to reason with him again and again, but
he seems to think he has the best of the argument.
No, Nat, I shall not tell you what the habit is,—
you will find out soon enough after you get there,
I'm afraid. But I'm going to trust my boy to the
promptings of his own conscience; for I am sure
he will be brave enough to do what he knows to be
right. Only, Nat, my boy, whenever you are tempted
to do wrong, never forget to lift up your heart to
God for help and for courage to do the right. And
don't forget that even a boy may sometimes be able
to do great good by his example."

Nat was somewhat mystified, but soon forgot all
about his mother's conversation, in the excitement
of preparing for the journey.

At last Christmas came; and Nat found himself
aboard the flying train. His uncle was at the train
to meet him, and what a welcome he received!
Everyone seemed glad to see him, and to be anxious
to give him a pleasant visit. Uncle Nathan lived
near the sea, and oh, how Nat loved the sea! It
seemed that he would never tire watching the
great white-caps toss and foam and chase each other
to the pebbly beach.

When supper was ready, Nat's place was beside
his uncle. Now Nat was a strict temperance boy;
he wore the blue-ribbon badge very proudly, for he
had signed the pledge. So when several bottles of
wine were brought in and placed on the table, he
looked inquiringly into his uncle's face.

"Oh, it's all right, my lad; it can't hurt you a

12

bit. You see, you need it, after the long, cold ride, to warm you up!"

"But don't you see my blue ribbon, Uncle Nathan? I've signed the pledge, and I can't drink wine."

"Oh! but I think it's quite ridiculous for a little shaver like you to sign the pledge, like some old toper!" and Uncle Nathan leaned back in his chair and laughed.

Poor Nat's face grew very red. He did not like to be called a "little shaver"—because he was twelve years old. And besides he *did* hate to have Uncle Nathan laugh at him. He wondered if it *would* do any harm *just once* to taste of a small glass of wine with his uncle.

Then quick as a flash he remembered his mother's words. Ah, so *this* must be the bad habit to which she had referred.

"Come," insisted Uncle Nathan, moving the sparkling liquid a little nearer his plate. "Come, Nat, be a man! you ought to be able to drink a little wine without getting drunk!"

Now Nat's one ambition was to be a man. Maybe Uncle Nathan was right after all.

"Even a boy may sometimes do great good by his example;" these were his mother's words. How plainly he remembered them! Nat's resolution was quickly formed. He wavered no longer.

"I've signed the pledge, Uncle Nathan, and if I can't be a man without breaking my word, why, I suppose I'll have to be a boy, then, as long as I live!"

Nat had a pretty hard fight before he could bring himself to oppose Uncle Nathan in this manner, but the voice of conscience was growing louder every moment, and with a silent prayer to Heaven for help to do right, Nat continued : —

"I tell you this, Uncle Nathan, if everybody would sign the pledge and keep it, there would be no drunkards any more, and there would be fewer prisons and poor-houses, and ever so much less misery in the world; that's what my father says."

The longer Nat thought about it, and the more he said, the stronger grew his conviction that he was doing right.

Uncle Nathan only smiled and gently patted Nat's shoulders. "Good boy; good boy," he smiled, "but we will see how you hold out."

One evening they were all going on a sleigh ride to the country to listen to a speech from a very noted gentleman. The evening was a bitter cold one, and the crisp snow sparkled like diamonds as the bright moonlight fell upon it.

Sleigh Ride to the Temperance Lecture

"Come, my lad," said Uncle Nathan, just as they were ready to start, "it's a stinging evening. Here's a little glass of sweetened toddy for you, just to keep you warm. I've had a nice glass, and I feel better and warmer already."

"I'm good and warm now, Uncle Nathan, and I don't need it. Besides, that stuff doesn't keep people warm,—it makes them cold. My father says he saw a man who froze to death just because he'd taken too much of that kind of stuff. When I have to die, Uncle Nathan, I don't mean to die that way."

Uncle Nathan smiled a little, called Nat a stubborn lad, and they all drove away.

Oh! how Nat *did* hope that the great gentleman whom they were going to hear, would say a few words—just a few at least—in favor of temperance; for Nat felt as if he needed a little help. He was tired of standing alone, as he thought. But if we are doing right, we are never alone. God is on our side, and His holy angels are with us.

Much to Nat's delight, the speaker gave most of the evening to explaining the evils of intemperance. He told of the misery and wretchedness caused by the liquor traffic. He spoke of the bright, promising young men of the nation, who were being led away from purity and right, and held in the hateful bondage of the cup. He spoke feelingly of the thousands of widows and tens of thousands of poor orphans all over our fair land, whose husbands and fathers had been murdered by the demon—drink.

At the close of his lecture, the speaker presented

the Pledge. And what was Nat's delight, when he saw his Uncle Nathan walk to the desk and sign his name,—and hark! Nat could hardly believe his ears! What *was* Uncle Nathan saying? What *did* he mean? Was it actually true?

"I have been much interested in the lecture this evening," began Uncle Nathan, "and am glad to place my name on the Pledge. I only wish it had been there long ago. As I have said, the lecture of the evening has been good; but friends, the

Uncle Nathan Signs the Pledge

greatest temperance lecture I ever listened to, has been given to me and acted out every day for the past week, by my young nephew, Nat Raymond. He is here to-night, and I wish to tell him that his influence, more than anything else in the world, has led me to take this stand."

"Hurrah for Nat Raymond!" broke out a dozen sturdy voices. And before he fairly understood what was going on, Nat found himself quite a hero.

At last, when his visit at Uncle Nathan's was over, and Nat was again at home, he told the story over and over to his happy parents.

"I never would have had the courage to refuse to take the wine with Uncle Nathan, mother," he declared, "if I had not remembered what you whispered in my ear the last thing before I left you: '*Don't forget, my son, that even a boy may be able to do great good by his example.*'"

"We can trace four-fifths of the crimes committed to the influence of rum."—*Judge Allison.*

"No business more thoroughly demoralizing, more destructive of public morals, public order, and public decency."—*Judge John Martin.*

"Seventy-five percent of the crimes of New York City are due directly or indirectly to strong drink."—*I. Kenny Ford, New York Police Court.*

"Seventy-five percent of accidents to life and limb due directly to drink."—*Dr. Cyrus Edson.*

"The undoubted cause of four-fifths of all the crime, pauperism, and domestic misery of the State."—*Governor Dix, of New York.*

"The chief source and immediate cause of more hurt to society and to individuals than any other agency."—*Hon. H. W. Blair.*

"The original cause of most of the enormities committed by criminals."—*Sir Matthew Hale.*

TOM'S TEMPERANCE LECTURE

IT WAS a bright autumn morning. The fall term of St. Rudolph's school had begun on Wednesday. Out on the playground, Tom Hadden,— a boy who had arrived only the night before,— was standing by himself, and looking about with the curious but sober eyes of a boy who felt as if he were in a new world, and who was as yet extremely doubtful as to his chances for happiness in that world.

"Hello, Tom Hadden; is that you?" some one called suddenly.

Tom's gloomy face brightened, and he turned eagerly toward a group of boys near him, who were talking and laughing in the manner so expressive at once of good comradeship and much self-importance,—a common characteristic of the older students at the beginning of a new school year.

Tom knew several of those boys; he had met them during the summer vacations, and their greetings now were so hearty that in a few minutes he forgot that he was that forlorn creature, a strange boy in a large school; and he gladly accepted an invitation to join his new friends after school hours, in a tramp over the hills to a village a short distance from St. Rudolph's.

In high spirits they set out; the hills were crossed, and they soon reached the village,

"Now for Cruger's," shouted several of the boys as they led the way to a saloon and boisterously pushed open the door.

Tom held back.   He did not like the appearance of the place.

"What are we going in here for?" he asked.

"For a spread, of course," one of the boys explained. "They cook great dinners here; come on."

Tom was quite ready for a "spread," and willingly followed the boys into a little back room where the saloon proprietor assured them they would be undisturbed. Their dinner was soon served, and thoroughly enjoyed by the hungry boys; then a dessert of fruit, cake, and pie was ordered, and when the last crumb of the last cake had disappeared, and the waiter had removed the dishes from the table, Frank Jones, their acknowledged leader, said gayly:—

"Now, fellows, before we go, we'll have a loving cup."

"A loving cup? what's that?" Tom asked of the boy nearest him.

"You needn't be afraid of it, it won't hurt you; it's only beer," the boy answered.

"Beer? I don't want any," and Tom pushed back his chair.

"Sit still; you can't go yet," said Frank Jones, and at that moment the waiter returned with the black bottles of beer.

Amid shouts of laughter the corks were drawn, and then one of the boys started the song:—

> "And here's a hand, my trusty friend,
> A gie's a hand o' thine,
> And we'll take a right guid willie-wought,—"

"No, no," protested Tom Hadden earnestly, "this is wrong. I will not drink. Let me go."

The boys stopped singing. "So you are a killsport, are you?" one of them said scornfully.

"No, no," Tom cried, "but I can't drink. Let me go."

The beer was foaming in their glasses, but the boys left it untouched, while they stared at Tom.

"You are a fool, Tom," one of them said. "What harm can a glass of beer do you?"

"Come, Tom," coaxed another, "don't make a row about nothing; be a man and drink your beer."

"I won't," Tom said sharply. "Let me go."

"We aren't quite ready to let you go yet," Frank Jones said angrily. "You are a pretty fellow to kill sport in this way; and now if you won't drink, you shall give us a temperance lecture. If it is wrong to drink beer, you shall tell us why. Come, boys, pay attention. You will now listen to an address on temperance from the eloquent orator, Thomas Hadden."

"Hear! Hear!" shouted the boys derisively, and one of them called: "Stand him up on the table."

"I will tell you a story that belongs to my own life"

(186)

"Up with you," cried two of the strongest boys, as they seized Tom, and, unable to resist, he was forced to mount the table. With crimson face and something suspiciously like tears in his eyes, he faced his tormentors.

"I can't, boys," he faltered. "I can't talk to you."

"More shame to you, then, for spoiling our fun," growled one of the boys. "Come, you needn't think we'll let you off. If you won't drink beer, you shall give us some good reason for not drinking it. That's only fair. Come, be quick about it."

Tom Hadden waited a moment. Once or twice he swallowed hard, and his breath came in quick gasps. Suddenly he threw back his head and straightened himself.

"Boys," he said, in a clear voice, "I will tell you a story—a story that belongs to my own life."

"All right," said Frank Jones recklessly, but something in Tom's face made the other boys watch him in silence.

"Boys," Tom went on, in a tender, pathetic voice, "I knew a little boy once who had a beautiful home. He had a kind father and mother, and he loved them both so much that he could never tell which he loved the best.

"That little boy's father had always been a good man; but once, when he wasn't well, the doctor ordered him to drink beer, and he began to drink it, and—" Tom's voice was thrilling in its emphasis now—"he soon began to drink stronger things; and there came a time when that little boy's home was so changed from the lovely place it once was, that it seemed as if a fiend must live there.

"That little boy heard his father rave and curse like a madman,—and he *was* mad, for drink had made him so. That boy saw his mother struck down by his drunken father's hand."

There was a dead silence in that little room. The beer had ceased to foam, but not a boy had tasted it or noticed it.

"Boys," Tom's thrilling voice went on, "that little boy is a large boy now, and he is almost alone in the world, for his father and mother are both dead, and now he has no home."

No boy who heard it ever forgot the pathos of Tom's tone as he continued :—

"Do you wonder, boys, that standing by his

Tom Hadden's Vow

mother's grave, that boy looked up to heaven, and solemnly vowed never while he lived, to touch or taste the drink that made a madman of his father, ruined his home, and broke his mother's heart?"

"You will let me go now," he said, as he jumped down from his high place, and started for the door. With a rush, the boys gathered around him.

"Tom," said Frank Jones, "you are a hero. Why, I think you are braver than a soldier. I am proud of you, and I would do just like you if I were in your place." The boy stopped; a new thought had come to him. He looked around on his companions.

"Boys," he said earnestly, "It seems to me that what I would do if I were in Tom's place, I would better do now in my own place."

Perhaps the head master of St. Rudolph's was never in his long life more happily surprised than he was that evening, when six of his oldest and most influential boys called on him and asked to sign the temperance pledge.

Years have passed since that evening, and those boys have kept their pledge.

" He played in a quiet and subdued manner as if afraid "
(190)

A LITTLE CHILD SHALL LEAD THEM

TWO children were playing on a lawn in front of a pleasant cottage. Roses and honeysuckles climbed up the windows, smooth walks, bordered with flowers, ran through the lawn; and everything about the cottage and the grounds had an air of taste and comfort.

A little way off, and very different in appearance, stood another cottage; the lawn in front was overgrown with weeds, and the walks with coarse grass. The fence that enclosed the lawn was broken in many places, and the gate, held only by the lower hinge, stood half open and awry. No roses or vines hung their green and crimson curtains about the windows, or clambered up the porch. This cottage had once been white also, white as that before which the children were playing; but it was now dirty and soiled and looked forlorn and comfortless.

There was as much difference in the appearance of the children as in the two cottages. One was neatly and cleanly dressed, and had a happy face. The clothes of the other were poor and soiled, and his face pale and sad. One played with hearty enjoyment, laughing and shouting; the other in a quied and subdued manner, as if afraid to raise his voice, in the happy sports of childhood.

"Jim, isn't that your father?" asked the well-dressed boy, as a man appeared coming down the road a little way off.

Jim started in a half-scared manner, and turned toward the road. He stood very still for a moment or two, looking at the man, and then, with a face now red, and now very pale, hurried away and laid himself close down upon the grass under some currant bushes, whispering as he did so, in a choking voice: —

"Don't, Freddy, please don't tell him I'm here."

Light and joy went out of Freddy's face also. He understood too well what all this meant.

Staggering down the road came Mr. Harwood, Jim's father.

What a sight it was! As he drew nearer, Freddy Wilson saw his red and swollen face, and heard him muttering and cursing to himself, and he shuddered with horror.

As Mr. Harwood passed the gate, he saw Freddy, and stopped. Freddy began to tremble. His first thought was to run back to the house; but he was a brave little boy, and it went against his feelings to run away from anything. So he did not move.

"Is my boy, Jim, here?" asked Mr. Harwood, in an angry voice. Some men, when drunk, are always ill-natured and cruel, and Jim's father was one of these. Seeing Freddy, and knowing that the two boys played much together, he naturally thought of his son.

Freddie did not answer.   He could not tell a lie, and so he said nothing.

"Did you hear me?" growled Mr. Harwood.

Still Freddy looked at him and said nothing. He knew that if Jim's father found him there, he would kick and beat him all the way home.   Not because the child had disobeyed his father, or was in any mischief, but Mr. Harwood, as I have said, was full of anger and cruelty when drunk, and took a savage pleasure in abusing his little boy.

Freddy began to be brave now, because he wished to save his little playmate from harm.

There was a bolt on the inside of the gate near which the child was standing.   With a stealthy motion, he slipped this bolt and fastened the gate. It was not done an instant too soon, for Mr. Harwood, growing furious, made a dash toward the boy, and tried to get at him through the gate.

"You young dog!" he growled, "I'll teach you manners!   Why don't you answer me?   Where's Jim?"

The drunken man shook the gate violently, and tried, with his unsteady hands, to find the bolt on the inside.   But his efforts were in vain.   He could not reach the little fellow, who stood up close to him, with a brave but sorrowful face. "You'd better go home, sir; I'll tell my father of this."

There was a manly firmness in the manner of the child, as well as in his words, that had their effect upon the drunken man.

13

"Who cares for your father? I don't!" he replied, moving back a step or two from the gate, muttering and cursing.

"But I say, youngster!" and he staggered a little nearer, with a scowl on his disfigured face, "just answer me one thing. Say yes or no. Is that young scamp of mine here?"

"I don't know any young scamp of yours, Mr. Harwood."

"You don't, eh! Now that's cool for a model young gentleman, like Master Wilson. Don't you know my Jim?"

"I know your Jim very well," said Freddie. "But he's a good little boy, and not a young scamp; and I don't think you're a kind father to call him such an ugly name."

This rebuke was felt by Mr. Harwood, drunk as he was. He could not endure the steady, fearless glance of Freddy's blue eyes. Then, away down in his heart, almost covered up and lost, was an old feeling of fatherly pride, and this was stirred at the praise spoken about Jim,—"a good little boy."

The anger went out of Mr. Harwood's face.

"He was a good little boy once," said he, with something so like tenderness in his voice, that Jim, who was lying close by, hidden under the currant bushes, sobbed aloud.

"What's that?" asked Mr. Harwood, leaning forward and looking toward the currant bushes. But the sound was hushed in a moment.

"He's a good little boy now," said Freddy,

speaking in a very firm voice and not seeming to hear the sob. "A good little boy," he repeated; and added, to make his assertion stronger, "there isn't a better one anywhere about here, and you let him go ragged, when he ought to have good clothes like the rest of us."

Mr. Harwood didn't stop to hear anything further, but turned from the gate and hurried toward the poor cottage across the road, walking more steadily than he had done a few minutes before. Then Freddy went behind the currant bushes where Jim still lay on the ground.

"He's gone," said Freddy.

The pent up grief in Jim's sad heart could be restrained no longer. He burst into a wild fit of crying that continued for several minutes. Freddy said all that he could to comfort his little friend; and when he had grown calm, asked with all the earnestness of a grown-up man : —

"Can't something be done, Jim?"

Jim shook his head in a hopeless way.

"Something ought to be done, and I am sure something *could* be done, if we only knew what it was. Oh! isn't drinking an awful thing!"

"It's the worst thing in the world," sobbed Jim. "When father is sober," he went on, "he's just as kind as he can be; but when he's drunk — O dear! it's dreadful to think of."

"Does he get drunk often?" asked Freddy.

"Now he does. He's drunk 'most all the time. But it wasn't so always. O dear! He used to be so good to us," he sobbed, "and take us out with him sometimes, and buy us nice things. He never does now. Most all of the money he gets, he spends at the tavern. But I must run home. Mother is almost sick, and father is so cross when he's been drinking; and she's weak and can't bear it," and Jim's tears ran over his cheeks again.

"Aren't you afraid he'll beat you?" asked Freddy.

"May be he will, and may be he won't," answered Jim. "But I must not stop to think of that. Mother is sick and weak, and father will be cross to her," and Jim hurried away.

All at once Freddy remembered how his defense and praise of Jim had cooled Mr. Harwood's anger, and he said to himself: "May be I can do some good,—and keep Mr. Harwood from beating poor Jim, or—"

But Freddy didn't stop to reason the case any longer, but hurried after his young friend, resolved to face the drunken man again in the hope of turning away his wrath.

The two lads entered Jim's poor home together, and stood face to face with Mr. Harwood.

"O father!" exclaimed Jim, as he saw, with glad surprise, a look of almost tender pity on his father's face; and as the child spoke, he sprang forward and caught his father's hand, clinging to it tightly.

This was too much for Mr. Harwood, who was not yet sober enough to control his feelings, and he turned away with a choking sob, trying to draw his hand out of Jim's; but the boy would not let

go his hold.   And now Freddy spoke out in behalf
of his little friend.

"Jim's a good boy, Mr. Harwood.   I know all
the boys around here, and there isn't one of them
better than Jim.   Father says so too; and lets me
have him over at our house whenever I please."

"Who said he wasn't a good boy," answered Mr.
Harwood, turning around upon Freddy with a half
angry manner.   I'd just like to hear anybody speak
against him, I would.

"He sprang forward and caught his father's hand"

And he sat down, drawing Jim between his knees
as he spoke.

A pale, thin, half-frightened woman, Jim's
mother, wondering what all this could mean, came
into the room.   Her eager eyes ran hurridly from
face to face.

"Don't be scared, Ellen," said Mr. Harwood,

"There isn't anything wrong. I'm only having a talk with these boys."

He was almost sober now. Excitement had cleared his stupid brain. Looking from one to the other of the lads, he could not help noticing the painful contrast; one so clean and well dressed, the other soiled and ragged.

He knit his brows closely, and sat very still, like one arguing for himself.

"I'll tell you what it is, mother," said he, turning his eyes toward Mrs. Harwood, "I'm not going to have our Jim running about, looking like a beggar's child. He's just as good as any of the boys around here, and I'll not have him ashamed to be seen with the best of them. I will drink nothing stronger than coffee, while I live, God being by helper!"

"Oh, thank God!" exclaimed the poor woman, dropping upon her knees and clasping her husband's neck. "Oh, thanks be to God!" she repeated. "He will be your helper. In Him is all compassion and all strength; but without Him our poor resolves are as nothing."

Freddy stood looking on for a little while, greatly moved by what was passing, then he walked quietly to the door and was going out, when Mr. Harwood called to him:—

"Just one word before you go. I'm sorry to say it; but it's in my thought now, and I feel that it would better come out. May be I wouldn't say it another time."

Freddy stopped and turned toward Mr. Harwood.

"I'm sorry to say it, Freddy, I am, for you are a nice boy, and have always been good to Jim.   But you'll thank me for it, may be, some of these days."

There was something in Mr. Harwood's manner that sent a feeling of alarm to Freddy's heart   He stood still, waiting, every pulse-beat sounding in his ears.

"May be your father's head is stronger than mine was five years ago," said Mr. Harwood, "but I've seen him at the "Black Horse" too often of late, going on just as I began.   It isn't safe, Freddy!   It isn't safe, and I don't like to see him there.   Look what I have come to!   But there was a time when

"I will not believe it"

I could hold my head as high as Mr. Wilson or anybody else in the neighborhood."

Freddy waited to hear no more.   It seemed as if night had fallen suddenly on his young spirit, and as if the air would suffocate him.   He turned and ran wildly away, such a weight and pain in his heart, that it seemed as if he would die. Mr. Wilson was coming along the road, and was near his own gate, when he saw Freddy hurrying across from Mr. Harwood's cottage, his face white as a sheet and strongly agitated.

"My son! what ails you?" he cried in alarm.

"O father!" was all that Freddy could say, as he stopped before him, and looked up with a strange, frightened face.

"I will not believe it," he sobbed, bursting into tears and hiding his face in his father's hands. "It's all a lie of Mr. Harwood's!"

"Won't believe what? my boy,— what has happened to grieve you so? A lie of Mr. Harwood's? What has that drunken wretch dared to say?" His voice changed to an angry tone.

"I can't tell you, father. It would choke me, but it's all a lie. Oh, I wish I hadn't said anything about it! But I felt so miserable, and you came right on me."

Mr. Wilson led Freddy within the gate to a seat under one of the trees.

"Now, my son," he said in a kind, firm voice, "tell me just what Mr. Harwood said."

Freddy then related all about the drunken man coming to the gate, and what had occured there, and all that he saw and heard when he went home with Jim, and at last he sobbed out the awful, warning words of Mr. Harwood.

As Freddy came to this last part, Mr. Wilson

turned his face so far away that his son could not
see it; but he felt his father's arm that was around
him clasp him more tightly. Then Mr. Wilson
placed his lips fondly and with a long pressure, on
Freddy's forehead.

"I will talk with Mr. Harwood about this," he
said in subdued tones, as they rose and went toward
the house.

Mr. Wilson went to see Mr. Harwood that very
day. Their interview was affecting to both, and
good for both. The warning words had not come
a moment too soon, and Mr. Wilson felt this so
deeply that he could not be angry with his poor
friend.

No one ever saw either of them at the "Black
Horse" after that, nor did they ever again permit
the cup of confusion to come near their lips.

PROHIBITION

THERE is a cause for the moral paralysis upon society. Our laws sustain an evil which is sapping their very foundations. Many deplore the wrongs which they know exist, but consider themselves free from all responsibility in the matter. This can not be. Every individual exerts an influence in society. In our favored land, every voter has some voice in determining what laws shall control the nation. Should not that influence and vote be on the side of temperance and virtue? The advocates of temperance fail to do their whole duty unless they exert their influence, by precept and example, by voice and pen and vote, in behalf of prohibition and total abstinence. We need not expect that God will work a miracle to bring about this reform, and thus remove the necessity for our exertion. We ourselves must grapple this giant foe, our motto, "No compromise," and no cessation of our efforts till victory is gained.—*Mrs. E. G. White.*

Does Prohibition Prohibit?

"'Prohibition doesn't prohibit!' That phrase has been worn threadbare by friends of the liquor traffic. They claim that as much liquor is sold in 'dry' districts as in 'wet.' Yet they do not look with indifference upon the strides made by prohibition; they are working as if the very life of their business depended upon the defeat of the temperance forces. And it probably does; for every

(202)

distillery, brewery, and saloon must have a license before its doors can swing open for business. In France the liquor dealers found it most profitable to have no prohibition law; for when the government granted liberty to the liquor trade, the consumption of alcohol increased nearly one hundred percent."— *Temperance Torchlights.*

Some Results of Prohibition

"I consider the prohibition law in Kansas as worth more to the railroad men than any other one thing."—*Superintendent of Santa Fe Railroad.*

"The five 'wettest' counties of West Virginia have four hundred fifteen convicts; the other fifty counties have four hundred thirteen. One-eleventh of the counties furnish one-half of the convicts."— *Statistics of 1909.*

"There is more hypocritical, illegal selling in license States than in Maine; for every joint or blind tiger under prohibition in Maine, there are sixteen blind tigers in licensed New York, plus twenty-seven thousand State licensed saloons."— *Mrs. Lillian M. N. Stevens.*

"Atlanta, at the end of 1908, showed 3,903 fewer arrests for drunkenness, and 8,102 fewer arrests for disorderly conduct—200 fewer juvenile arrests." — *Mrs. Mary Harris Armor.*

"One-third of our counties are without prisoners in their jails or paupers in their almshouses; one-half of our counties sent *no convicts* to our prisons this year, and one-half of our prison inmates never lived in Kansas long enough to acquire a residence here. Churches and schools flourish, the spiritual outlook is hopeful, and the saloon is practically banished."— *Governor Hoch, of Kansas, in his Thanksgiving Message.*

ATLANTA, GEORGIA.— "For the first time in its fifteen years of existence, every cell at the police jail yesterday afternoon was empty. Not a prisoner was incarcerated, and the turnkeys and matrons were having a very dull afternoon. The police attribute this remarkable condition to the prohibition law which went into effect the first day of the year."—*Washington Times, Jan. 25, 1908.*

———

"Without one dollar of revenue from the saloon, Maine has a larger percentage of the total population in the public schools than any other of the New England States, or New York, with its twenty million dollars of revenue from the saloon. It has more teachers employed in proportion to the school population than any other State.

"It is stated by Lady Henry Somerset that in one district in Liverpool, England, in which there is no saloon, there is but one pauper to every one thousand inhabitants. In another district, in which there are two hundred saloons, there is one pauper to every twenty-eight inhabitants.

"Abyssinia has prohibition, and the penalty for taking liquors into that country is death. In the capital of the country only two murders have been committed in the last forty years. Smoking is also prohibited."— *Temperance Torchlights.*

CIGARETTE POISON

"You smoke thirty cigarettes a day?"

"Yes, on the average."

"Are they to blame for your run-down condition?"

"Not in the least. I blame my hard work."

The physician then took a leech out of a glass jar.

"Let me show you something," he said. "Bare your arm."

The cigarette fiend bared his pale arm, and the other laid the lean, black leech upon it. The leech fell to work busily, its body began to swell. Then, all of a sudden, a kind of shudder convulsed it, and it fell to the floor dead.

"That is what your blood did to that leech," said the physician.

"I guess it wasn't a healthy leech, any way."

"Wasn't healthy, eh? Well, we'll try again."

And the physician clapped two leeches on the young man's thin arm.

"If they both die," said the patient, "I'll swear off—or at least, I'll cut down to ten a day."

Even as he spoke, the smaller leech shriveled and dropped on his knee, dead, and a moment later the larger one fell besides it.

"This is ghastly," said the young man; "I'm worse than the pestilence to these leeches."

"It is the empyreumatic oil in your blood," said the medical man. "All cigarette fiends have it."

"Doc," said the young man, regarding the three dead leeches thoughtfully, "I half believe you're right."— *Evanston* (*Illinois*) *Index*.

MADE A DRUNKARD BY HIS CIGAR

I KNEW a young clergyman whose oratory obtained for him the admiration of many influential persons, among whom was a gentleman of fortune, who courted his company and taught him to smoke.

The young minister was warned of his danger, but could not be persuaded to renounce that which he considered a harmless indulgence. He insisted that his cigar soothed his mind and composed his feelings. A friend, in reply, told him that the mind never needs composing when in health; and the feelings never need artificial soothing only when improperly irritated; and added, "Beware how you indulge in a bad habit."

Impatient under the rebuke, the clergyman replied: "I smoke but seldom, and could almost do without it."

'Seldom' and 'almost' are two fatally ominous words. 'Seldom' will become 'regular,' and 'almost' be converted into 'always.' And as smoking and drinking are companions, let me beseech

you, said his friend, "not to make them yours.
Ministers should be a fence around the pit of per-
dition.

"Some inexperienced youth may see you smoke,
and, imitating your example, become a confirmed
smoker, and sooner or later a confirmed drunkard.
The line of demarkation being once effaced, he
may soon be lost in the vortex of sin."

Little did this young preacher suppose this to be
a prophetic picture of his own mournful case. But
he continued the habit, and, little by little, his
splendid talents became dim, and his hearers for-
sook him. His wealthy host, who first taught him
to smoke, witnessed his growing desire for stimulants, and with a look more expressive than words,
declared that "in spite of praying and preaching,
professors of religion like the good things of this
life, as well as others; and that, after all, saints and
sinners are pretty much alike."

The days of this eloquent young clergyman were
ended in ignominy; and a life which promised to
be happy and illustrious, was early brought to a
miserable close. His intemperate habits, it was
supposed, killed his young wife, and made a beggar
of his child. He died in a madhouse, blaspheming
the very Saviour whom he had once preached.

Avoid smoking. "It is the devil's leading string,
beginning with a hair and ending with a cable."

DAVID PAULSON, M. D.
President Anti-Cigarette League of America

SLAUGHTER OF THE INNOCENTS

BY DAVID PAULSON, M. D.

IN the Bellevue Hospital Medical College, when I was a student, I performed an experiment that vividly impressed upon my mind the naked fact that nicotin is a deadly poison. A large, healthy cat had become such a nuisance that it was decided to kill it. This I proceeded to do by the following method: I soaked enough tobacco in water to make an ordinary cigarette. Then I injected under the cat's skin a hypodermic syringe full of this tobacco juice. In a few moments the cat began to quiver, then to tremble more violently, then it had cramps, and in less than twenty minutes it died in violent convulsions.

I take no pride in relating this experiment, for I know a shorter as well as a more merciful method of ending a cat's life.

But what interests me now is the truth that thousands of young men and boys are waking up to the fact that tobacco in any form, and cigarettes in particular, are unmitigated evils. And that for their own sakes, they cannot afford to introduce into their bodies that which only makes them weak, sickly, and useless.

I will tell you, briefly, how the burden of this terrible curse was rolled upon my heart. God used a never-to-be-forgotten incident to burn into my soul the tremendous importance of this cigarette evil.

One day, an old lady, with a faded red shawl thrown over her stooping shoulders, came into my office, and asked if I could see her boy. Two strong men then brought before me a poor boy of seventeen years, wild-eyed and insane. The mother asked if he could be cured.

After investigating the case, I was compelled to tell her that the outlook was hopeless, and that she might just as well send him to the lunatic asylum. She broke down and sobbed as though her heart would break. I asked her what had brought this terrible condition upon her son, and she said:—

"Oh, it was cigarettes. He began to smoke more and more, until he used fifty a day, and then his mind gave way."

That day I became thoroughly enlisted in the anti-cigarette war. O that our souls might become saturated with the importance of fighting this awful evil! Cigarettes are making our boys weak and puny and unmanly. They are sapping the strength from their muscles, and making them unable to win their way in the world.

I care not how intelligent or brainy a boy may naturally be, a short period of cigarette smoking will tell on him. He may not notice this himself,

at once, but others will. And I wish the young
men and boys to remember that if there is work to
be done in the world which requires much effort,
either of brain or muscle, the cigarette smoker is
not chosen for the job. Why?—Because when the
time comes to use the brain or the muscles for some
supreme effort, the poor, poison-soaked muscles fail
to respond, and the benumbed brain cannot do its
best work. I think if the boys only understood
that cigarettes and tobacco were ruining them physically and mentally, and preparing them for certain
defeat in life, they would shun both as they would
the plague.

The Cigarette Fiend Is an Object of Pity

When I talk on the cigarette evil in the Chicago
public schools, I ask how many of the children
know of some poor crippled boy whose leg was cut
off by a street-car accident. Such a boy, if he has
brains and character, may yet fill a position of trust
and usefulness in the world, but the boy who begins
to smoke cigarettes early enough, can never be of
any use in this world, and unless he repents, there
will be no place for him in the next. To try to
put knowledge into his brain, is as hopeless a task
as to try to fill a basket with water.

The cigarette-smoking boy is looked upon by
other people as an object of pity. There is nothing truly brave or heroic about him. There may
have been naturally, but nature has been doped and
stupefied and abused, until there is nothing left in
the poor lad that is manly at all. If he wants to

be a great hunter or a fine marksman or sharpshoot-

er, he must either give up this ambition, or else let the cigarette alone forever. If he would like to be a famous doctor or a skillful surgeon, he must not ruin his nerves, or he cannot trust himself to hold a surgeon's knife. No one would be willing to risk his life in such hands.

Listless Cigarette Smoker

Hang a half dozen brick around a boy's neck, and ask him to swim a race with you. Would that be fair? But the cigarette habit pulls one under in life's struggle, just the same.

What would the boys think if they saw a lad vigorously

Pumping Water into Basket

rubbing sand into his eyes? They would think

him crazy.   Is it any more foolish to rub sand into the eyes than it is to rub poison into the brain?

Suppose I should hand a boy my watch, and presently he begins to pour tar into its works. Would you think he had much sense?

O it is cruel and unmanly to ruin and clog up and destroy these wonderful bodies of ours.   What an astonishing piece of machinery the brain is! Almost everything depends upon having the head clear,— the reasoning powers sharp and acute.   But the deadly cigarette destroys the keen sensibility of the nerve and brain cells, and renders the victim unable to think clearly or logically.

Men who train great wrestlers and athletes to perform almost unbelievable feats of physical endurance, know better than to allow them to poison and paralyze these muscles of iron.   Who ever heard of an athlete smoking half a dozen cigarettes just before starting in to win his medal as champion?

Destroys on the Installment Plan

Who has not watched the old family cat and noticed

how she kills a mouse,— a little at a time,— crushing her teeth into the poor thing's body, then letting it limp away a short distance, then springing upon it and crushing it some

"The cigarette kills the boy in the same way."

more. Now the cigarette kills the boy in just the same way, or, in other words, on the installment plan.

Any experienced physician can pick out a cigarette slave almost as far as he can see him; for no one can smoke cigarettes a very long time, before he begins to have the devil's trade-mark stamped upon him.

We must never forget that we only pass over this road once,—we have but one life here to live; and when we reach the end of the journey, if the *Master* cannot say to us, "Well done," our life has been a hopeless failure.

A Simple but Sure Cure

But suppose you have in mind some poor fellow who has become enslaved by the unmanly habit. Of course you pity him in his helpless bondage. Well, you may assure him that he may be saved by living exclusively on a fruit diet for several days, eating all he wishes of it three or four times a day, drinking plenty of water, and availing himself of a sweat bath or two if convenient. I know from experience that God is on the side of the fellow who is trying to do right,—that he may look to Him for special help. Then the poor cigarette slave will be astonished to see that it *is* possible to slip out from under the yoke of habit.

Now in conclusion I want to say a few words to grown people who use tobacco. I have seen a father teach his boy to pray, to ride a bicycle, and to spell; but I never yet have seen a sensible,

respectable man teach his boy to smoke. This is
the best argument I know against tobacco using.
If a man really believed tobacco was good for him,
he would want his wife, or his sister, or his mother,
and his child to share with him in this blessing.

The Real Truth about Tobacco

Tobacco does give a certain amount of unearned
felicity, just as alcohol or morphin does; but it
charges a terrific toll in the way of high blood pressure, injury to the nervous system and the digestive
organs, and more or less impairment of the whole
man. Every man who is a tobacco user sacrifices
some of the best that is in him, spiritually, mentally, and physically. The intolerable craving for
the after-dinner cigarette is often produced by the
juicy beefsteak, highly spiced food, or tea and coffee, that compose the meal. Hence, he who would
be delivered from the tobacco habit, should religiously avoid such articles of food as create a demand
and an unnatural craving for tobacco.

But some will ask, "is it worse for a child to
smoke a cigarette than it is for a man to smoke a
cigar?"—Yes, for three reasons:—

First, a man may safely tolerate a quarter of a
grain of morphin, while we dare not give a child
more than a sixteenth part of a grain. A young
person's nervous system is peculiarly susceptible to
the influence of such narcotic drugs as nicotin and
morphin, and hence an introduction to either of
them early in life, spells almost certain disaster,
mental or nervous, later in life.

Second, the loosely packed cigarette does not permit the nicotin to condense to the same extent as when it is drawn through pipe or cigar; hence the smoker gets the full benefit(?)of this virulent poison.

Third, the oxidation of the cigarette paper produces deadly poison which is only second in its effects to that of nicotin itself.

Well, then, to sum up: Is it any wonder that so many thousands of our brightest, smartest, keenest young men and boys are signing the Cigarette Pledge? They are keen enough to see that cigarettes and tobacco used in any form, mean weak brains, flabby muscles, diseased heart, and a useless and unhappy life.

THE MAJOR'S CIGAR

AFTER a separation of many years, I met my old friend, Major————, at a railway station. If he had not spoken first, I should not have recognized my Virginia comrade of '64. It was not merely the disguise of a silken hat and a shaven cheek, but,—as I told him after we had chatted awhile about each other's ups and downs since the war,—I was sure this was the first time I had ever seen him away from the table, without a cigar in his mouth.

"Haven't smoked for five years," was his reply. "I'm down on tobacco as thoroughly as you ever were."

"Good. Tell me about it."

We locked arms, and walked leisurely up and down the platform. Dropping the dialogue, this was, in substance, his story.—

"It wasn't a sudden conversion. I never was quite so easy in my mind over it as I pretended to be. I intended to taper off when I got home from the army. And I did,—smoked less in three weeks than I used to in one.

"But one summer I went off on some business for our company, which kept me up in the mountains, among the charcoal burners, three days longer than I expected. I got out of cigars, and couldn't obtain any at any price.

"In forty-eight hours I was more uncomfortable and unstrung than I had ever been in my life. I actually borrowed an old Irishman's filthy clay pipe, and tried to smoke it. I though of that miserable summer we spent, crawling about the trenches in Virginia, and, I am ashamed to confess that I wished I was there again, with a cigar in my mouth.

"Then, I began to realize what a shameful bondage I was in to a mere self-indulgence. I, a man who secretly prided himself on his self-control, nerve, manliness,—who never flinched at hard fare or rough weather,—a downright slave to a bad habit; unnerved and actually unfit for business for lack of a cigar. It made me angry at myself; I despised myself for my weakness.

"Going into the matter a little further, I found that the money I had spent for cigars in a dozen years would have paid for my house and furnished it. I had smoked away more money than I had laid out for our library, our periodicals, and our intellectual culture generally. Cigars had cost me nearly twice as much as I had given to church work, missions, and charity.

"My conscience rose up at the record. I knew I could not plead any equivalent for the outlay; it

had not fed me; it had not strengthened me; it
had simply drugged me. Every cigar had made
the next cigar a little more necessary to my comfort. To use the mildest word, it had been a *useless* expenditure.

"My detention in the mountains was càlculated
to open my eyes to my domestic short-comings, and
I saw, as I never saw before, how selfishly unsocial
tobacco had made me at home. I smoked before I
was married, and
my wife never
entered any pro-
test against my
cigars afterward.

An Unsocial Habit

"But our first
baby was a ner-
vous child, and
the doctor told
me it would not do
for it to breathe
tobacco smoke.
So I got into the
way of shutting
myself up in the
library of even-
ings, and, after
meals, to enjoy my cigars. As I look at it now,
nothing is more absurd than to call smoking a
social habit. It's a poor pretense of sociability,
where a man is simply intent on his own enjoyment. My wife owns now that my tobacco-tainted

breath and tobacco-saturated clothing were always
more or less a trial to her.

"The satisfaction it has given me to be rid of a
tobacco atmosphere, and the thought of my contemptibly selfish indifference to her comfort all those
years. have humbled me, I tell you.   And I wouldn't
exchange my own daily
satisfaction now-a-days
in being a *cleaner* man
— inside and outside, —
for the delight that anybody gets out of his
cigars.

"I didn't need to go
outside of my own door
to find reasons enough
for giving up the habit;
but I think I found still
stronger ones, after all,
when I went away from
home.

"The more I thought
about the harm tobacco
does in the community
at large, the more sure
I felt that it was time
for me to stop giving
it the moral support of

The Smoking Doctor   my example.   I know
I smoked too much, and that my nervous system is
still the worse for it ; and I think the people who

are likely to be hurt the most by it, are just the ones who are most likely to smoke excessively.

"And then, I've noticed that the doctors who stand up for tobacco are always men who use it, and are liable to the suspicion of straining a point in justification of their own self indulgence

"On one point, though, I believe the authorities agree. No one denies that it is a damaging indulgence for boys. It means a good deal when smoking is forbidden to the pupils in the polytechnic schools of Paris, and the military schools of Germany, purely on hygienic grounds. The governments of these smoking nations are not likely to be notional in that matter.

"But the use of tobacco by our American boys and men is excessive and alarming. We ought to save our rising generation for better work than they can do if tobacco saps the strength of their growing years, and makes the descent easier, as it no doubt often does, to worse vices. I don't know how to forgive myself for the example I set before my Sabbath-school class of bright boys, year after year, by my smoking habits.

"It isn't in the family, either, that the selfishness of the habit is most apparent. I don't believe, other things being equal, that there is any other class of men who show such a disregard in public for other people's comfort as tobacco users do. A man would be considered a rowdy or a boor who would willingly spatter mud on the clothing of a lady as she passed him on the sidewalk. But a lady to whom tobacco fumes are more offensive than mud, can hardly walk the streets in these days, but that men who *call themselves gentlemen,*—and who are gentlemen in most other respects,—blow their cigar smoke into her face at almost every step.

"Smokers drive other men out of the gentlemen's cabins on the ferryboats, and from the gentlemen's waiting rooms in railroad stations, monopolizing these rooms as coolly as if they, only, had any rights in them.

"I can't explain such things except on the theory that tobacco beclouds the moral sense, and makes men especially selfish."

The Major's train came in just then, and as he took my hand to say "Good-by," the smoking car of the waiting train drew his parting shot.

"See there! did you ever reflect how the tobacco habit levies its taxes on everybody? The railway company furnishes an extra car for the smokers, which, in the nature of the case, must be paid for by an extra charge on the tickets of all the passengers. What a stir it would raise if the legislature should attempt to furnish luxuries to any special class at public cost in this way!

"How we'd vote them down! I vote against this thing by throwing away my cigar."

WHY HE DIDN'T SMOKE

OHNNIE LORD, the son of Mr. Jeremy Lord, aged fourteen, was spending the afternoon with one of his young friends, and his stay was prolonged into the evening, during which some gentlemen — friends of the family — dropped in.

The boys withdrew into the recess of the bay-window, while the men chatted sociably together.

The two boys kept their ears open, as boys will, and, taking their cue from the sentiments expressed by their elders, endorsed one or the other, as they happened to agree with them.

"Gentlemen, will you smoke?" asked Mr. Benedict, the host. A simultaneous, "thank you," went around, and a smile of satisfaction lighted every face but one. He was not gloomy or a drawback on the others, but his smile was not one of assent. A box of costly and fragrant (?) cigars was soon forthcoming.

"Fine cigar," said one, as he held it to his nose before lighting it. "What, Linton, you don't smoke?"

"I'm happy to say I do not," was the firm rejoinder.

"Well, now, you look like a smoking man, jolly, care free, and all that. I'm quite surprised," said another.

" It's driving her out of her house"

"We are hardly doing right to smoke in the
parlor, are we?" asked a red-faced man, puffing
away heartily. I yield that much to my wife's dislike of the weed. She makes a great ado about the
curtains, you know."

"For my part, that's a matter I don't trouble
myself about," said the host, broadly. "There's
no room in this house too good for me and my
friends to smoke in. My wife has always understood that, and she yields, of course."

"But you don't know how it chokes her," said
young Hal Benedict. "Yes, indeed, it gets all
through the house, you know, and she almost
always goes into Aunt Nellie's, when there are two
or three smoking. There she goes, now," he added,
as the front door shut.

"Why, it's absolutely driving her out of her
house, isn't it?" whispered Johnnie Lord, from
his nook. "Too bad!"

"Why don't you smoke, Linton?" queried one of
the party. "'Fraid of it? Given it up lately? Of
course it doesn't agree with some constitutions."

"Well, if you want to know why I don't smoke,
friend Jay," was the answer, "I will tell you; I
respect my wife too much."

"Why, you don't mean—" stammered his questioner.

"I mean simply what I said. When I was married, I had the habit of smoking cigars. But I saw
that the smoke annoyed her, though she behaved
with the utmost good taste and forbearance. See-
15

ing this, I cut down my cigars so as to smoke only when going to and returning from business.

"But even then, I considered what my presence must be to a delicate, sensitive woman, with my breath and clothes saturated with the odor, and I began to be disgusted with myself, so that I finally dropped the habit, and I can't say I'm sorry."

"I shouldn't be, I know," said another, admiringly. "I'm candid enough to own it, and I think your wife ought to be very much obliged to you."

"On the contrary, it is I who ought to be obliged to my wife," said Mr. Linton, while the host smoked on in silence, very red in the face, and evidently wincing under the reproof that was not meant.

"I say, Linton is a perfect gentleman," whispered young Benedict.

"He's splendid," supplemented Johnnie Lord, who was thinking his own thoughts; but the smoke was really getting too much for him, and presently he took his leave.

The next day Johnnie Lord was thoughtful; so quiet, indeed, that everybody noticed it. In the evening, when his father lighted his pipe, with its strong tobacco, Johnnie seemed to be on thorns.

"I can't think that you don't respect mother," he blurted out, and then his face grew scarlet.

"What do you mean?" asked his father in a severe voice. "I say, what do you mean, sir?"

"Because mother hates the smoke so; because it gets into the curtains and carpet—and—and—because I heard Mr. Linton say last night, that he did not smoke because he respected his wife too much."

"Pshaw! Your mother doesn't mind my smoking—do you mother?" he asked, jocularly, as his wife entered the room.

"Well—I—I used to, rather more than I do now. One can get accustomed to anything, I suppose, so I go on the principle that what can't be cured must be endured."

"Nonsense! you know I could stop to-morrow if I wanted to," he laughed.

"But you won't want to," she said, softly.

Now I don't know whether Johnnie's father gave up the weed. Most likely not; but if you want to see what really came of it, I will give you a peep at the following paper, written some years ago, and which happens to be in my possession.

"*I John Lord, of sound mind, do make, this first day of January, the following resolutions, which I pray God I may keep:* —

"*FIRST: I will not get married until I own a house.*

"*SECOND: I will never swear, because it is silly, as well as wicked.*

"*THIRD: I will never smoke, and so make myself disagreeable to everybody who comes near me, and I will always keep these words as my motto after I am married:* —

"'*I don't smoke because I respect my wife.*' *Mr. Linton said that, and I will never forget it.*"

And Johnnie kept his word like a hero.

EXPERIENCES OF JOHN B. GOUGH

HEN in Worcester, England, twenty-six years ago, I was the guest of a gentleman, a member of Parliament, who resided just opposite the city, on the bank of the river,—a delightful place.

I was at that time a smoker, and although I had never smoked in a gentleman's house without an invitation, I deemed it necessary to have my smoke after dinner, if I could get it without annoying others.

So, after dinner, I strolled down to the riverside, out of sight of the house, took out my cigars and matches and proceeded to light a cigar. The wind blew out the match. Another was tried, and another. I took off my hat to shield it from the wind. It was of no avail. I got some brimstone down my throat, or something as bad; but the cigar would not ignite.

Then I kneeled down close to the rock by the path, at the side of the river, and with my hat off, endeavored to secure the object. Now, I never go on my knees but I am reminded of prayer, and the thought came :—

"If anyone should see me, he would probably think that some man had sought that retired spot for devotion, and that he was saying his prayers;

and what am *I* doing?—I am sucking away at a
cigar, hoping to obtain fire enough from the match
to get a smoke. What would the audience say,
who heard me last night, if they should see me?"

The inconsistency of my practise with my profession struck me so forcibly that I said, "*I'll have
no more of it.*"

I rose from my knees, took the cigars and the
matches from my pockets, and threw them into the
river, and I never touched a cigar to smoke for
eighteen years.

The reformed drunkard, John B. Gough, who became the great evangelist of temperance, kept his
freedom from drink at the cost of occasional terrible
torture. To its awful intensity, an old friend, with
whom he made his home whenever he visited
Chicago, bears witness. The story contains not
only a vivid warning against drink, but a hopeful
illustration of the victories that, with God's help,
may be won.

"One day I found Mrs. Gough sitting by the
window, holding her newspaper upside down. Mr.
Gough was lying on the lounge on the other side
of the room, with his face to the wall.

"'What is the matter?' I asked in alarm.

"'What makes you think anything is the matter?' Mrs. Gough asked.

"With a gesture, I indicated the newspaper.

"'Oh, there *is* matter!' she cried. 'Go to John!'

"I sat down by him, and began to talk to him in

a low voice, while I smoothed his hair, as he loved to have me do because it soothed him. I reminded him of the good he was doing, of the thousands he had redeemed from drink, and of the families that he had made happy.

"All at once he turned over and looked at me. I hardly knew him! His eyes were sunken, his skin was ghastly gray. Then he said with the deep voice that so thrilled his audiences:—

"'Do you believe I love that woman over there by the window?'

"'I have never doubted it,' I replied.

"'Do you believe I love you?' he asked.

"'It is one of the chief joys of my life to know that you do,' I said, with a lump in my throat.

"'Then if you want to know how I feel,' he cried, 'It is this way: as if I'd be willing to see you both in hell, if it would only be right for me to take just one drink!'

"To such an extremity as this can the morbid craving for drink reduce even a good man. The temptation came upon him now and then with awful force. It was heart-breaking to see him. At such times he never dared to be left alone. Once when he was thus attacked by temptaion at a hotel away from his friends, he locked the door of his room and threw the key out over the transom.

"'Once the devil gets a cluch on you, he never lets go,' he said. 'God save our young people from thinking that the habit is only a little thing!'"

TALMAGE ON TOBACCO

A T a Friday evening lecture in New York City, Dr. Talmage spoke on the evil habit of tobacco using, as follows : —

"There are a multitude of young men smoking themselves to death. Nervous, cadavorous, narrow-chested, and fidgety, they are preparing for early departure, or a half-and-half existence that will be of little satisfaction to themselves, or of little use to others. Quit it, my young brother. Before you get through this life, you will want stout nerves and a broad chest and a brain unclouded with tobacco smoke.

"To get rid of the habit will require a struggle, as I know by bitter experience. Cigars and midnight study nearly put an end to my existence at twenty-five years of age. I got so I could do no kind of study without a cigar in my mouth—as complete a slave as some of you are.

"At one time I was about to change pastorates from one city to another, when a wholesale cigar dealer offered as an inducement to my going to Philadelphia, that he would give me all my cigars, free of charge, all the rest of my life. He was a

(231)

splendid man, and I knew he would keep his promise.

"Then I reasoned thus: If now, when my salary is small, and cigars are high, I smoke up to my full endurance, what would become of my health if I got all of my cigars for nothing? Well, I have never touched the infernal weed since. From that time I was revolutionized in health and mind,—emancipated by the grace of God.

"I implore young men to strike out for the liberation of their entire nature from all kinds of evil habits. Even on our railroads they have introduced a pig-pen on wheels,—the smoking-car—and it is being made easier and easier all of the time to sacrifice physical strength and health.

"All those who break down their health through indulgence, and go into the grave sooner than they would otherwise have done, are suicides, and the day of judgment will so reveal it."

———

A prominent church man once said: "I used to use tobacco. When I gave it up I had a hard time for ten weeks. I was unable to sleep at night, would walk the floor, but God gave me the victory."

Dr. Cole, a prominent Methodist physician, said: "I used to use the weed, but I reached the time when I wanted to lead a better spiritual life, and I felt that tobacco stood between my Maker and my soul."

TOBACCO AND THE CIGARETTE

PART ONE — WHAT IS TOBACCO?

"Tobacco is the worst curse of modern civilization."—John Ruskin.

WHILE the pages of this book are devoted largely to the drink evil, we must not forget the monster evil of Tobacco, nor of the small, innocent appearing Cigarette. For although small singly, in the aggregate it is appalling. From year to year the consumption of Cigarettes has so rapidly increased, that in 1911 there were 11,250,000,000 consumed in the United States alone. Of the track of ruin left by this "little monster," the following pages will testify.

So close a second does the evils of Tobacco run to that of drink, that it is claimed by many that Tobacco is a greater curse than Rum. But one fact is sure: Tobacco in all its forms, more than all other influences, creates a thirst for alcoholic drinks, and is the greatest friend of the saloon.

The data from which this department has been compiled, was supplied by a lecturer on the Cigarette evil of more than four years' experience. His facilities for obtaining accurate information, and important statements from reliable sources, have been unsurpassed.

We commend the facts presented in this department to the careful consideration of every one into whose hands this book may fall.

What is Tobacco? It is a poison so deadly that it cannot be brought under the Pure Food and Drug Act. It is not rated as a drug, but as a poison too dangerous to use in ordinary medical practice. It can be brought under the Drug Act only by special action of Congress. Please note what medical men say of it : —

"Tobacco is the *most subtle* poison known to the chemist, except the deadly prussic acid."—*M. Orfila, President of the Medical Academy, Paris.*

"It is believed by all judicious practitioners *too dangerous* to be employed as a medicine. The benefits as a remedy do not counterbalance the risk of using it. Yet so insidious are its effects that few have regarded it as swelling the bills of mortality. It is, nevertheless, true that *multitudes* are carried to the *grave* every year by *tobacco* alone."— *Dr. Grimshaw*

"Surgeons have sometimes resorted to a weak infusion of tobacco injected into the bowels in cases in which it was necessary to induce immediate prostration of energy, as in cases of strangulated hernia and in bad dislocations of the joints; but even in these cases, the risk is so great that no prudent surgeon will use it except as a last resort."—Dr. Harris.

" The profession have no idea of the ignorance of the public regarding the nature of tobacco. Even intelligent, well-educated men stare in astonishment when wou tell them it is one of the most powerful poisons. Now is this right? Has the medical profession done its duty? Ought we not as a body to have told the public that of all our poisons, it is the most insidious, uncertain, and, in full doses, the most deadly?"—Dr. Solly, Insurance Medical Examiner.

" One-fourth of a drop of nicotin will kill a frog in ten seconds; one-sixth of a drop will kill a cat in fourteen seconds."

"The poison is slow; but in the second and third decade its virus becomes manifest. The words of the wise man, "Because sentence against an evil work is not executed speedily, therefore the heart of the sons of men is fully set in them to do evil," is strikingly applicable to those who indulge in this pernicious habit. There have died in New York, within a few years, three excellent clergymen, all of whom might now have been alive, had they not used tobacco. The duty of abstaining from the slow killing of one's self by this poison is as clear as the duty of not cutting one's throat."—Dr. Willard Parker.

" Tobacco is not an innocent substance. It contains nicotin, an alkaliod which is a poison, destroying life very quickly, even when taken in small doses. It acts as speedily as hydrocyanic [prussic] acid. Thirty grains of tobacco, or one or two drops of nicotin, would most likely be a fatal dose. Death by tobacco may occur in less than half an hour; by the alkaloid [nicotin] in a few minutes."—Norman Kerr, M. D.

" So very dangerous and potent are its narcotic properties, that tobacco is only seldom used for any purpose in medicine; and when it is resorted to, the greatest caution is necessary."—Dr. Elisha Harris.

" The profession have no idea of the ignorance of the public regarding the nature of Tobacco. Even intelligent, well-educated men stare in astonishment when you tell them it is one of the most powerful poisons. Now is this right? Has the medical profession done its duty? Ought we not as a body to have told the public that of all our poisons, it is the most insidious, uncertain, and, in full doses, the most deadly?" — Dr. Solly, Insurance Medical Examiner.

TOBACCO AND THE CIGARETTE

PART TWO — ECONOMIC

WHY do farmers raise Tobacco, manufacturers make it up, and dealers sell it? — It is because there is an enormous profit in it all along the lines. The profit is so great that the manufacturers sometimes pay $1500.00 to $2000.00 for a single advertisement in a leading journal.

In an editorial entitled "The Damnable Cigarette," in the *Religious Weekly*, of May 6, 1911, we read of the profits of the Tobacco Trust as follows: —

" The evil is fearfully profitable.—the net income over $25,000,000 —an increase of about twenty per cent. The dividends on common stock increased from fifty per cent to sixty-two and one-half per cent. The fat pockets of the recipients jingled with the gruesome coin, while insane lads and weeping mothers sat in sodden shame and sorrow."

What Statistics Show

" The consumers of chewing and smoking tobacco, in 1908, paid as a tax into the United States Treasury at the rate of $54,984 per day. *They more than paid the sailors of the United States Navy.*"

" The smokers of *cigars* and *Cigarettes* pay an average of *sixty-six thousand six hundred thirty-seven dollars per day* in tax, or enough to provide salaries for the Supreme Court of the United States for one whole year. And the good 'Sisters of the Chimney Corner' paid *tax on snuff* at the rate of *three thousand four hundred seventy-three dollars a day.* They thus contribute enough money to Uncle Sam's exchequer, to maintain the Public Health and Marine hospital service."

" Should three of our largest American cities burn down each year, it would be considered a national calamity; and yet, each year, the people of this country burn up in tobacco leaves, an amount equal to the total assessed valuation of Detroit, Cincinnati, and Buffalo. But the financial waste is of small consideration compared with the physical and moral waste resulting therefrom."

"*A brand new Panama Canal* could be built each year for the money that is reduced to ashes between the lips of America's cigar smokers. And the census report shows that the consumption of cigars since 1860 has increased *twenty-fold*, while the population has increased only *twofold*. Every year our cigar bill increases another thirty million dollars."

" An industry that shows such stupendous figures of present volume and of steady growth, indicates unusual stability."

(235)

Dr. D. H. Kress, speaking from his extended experience as physician and superintendent of sanitariums in England, in Australia, and in America, where he has had unusual opportunities for observing the effect of tobacco upon the human body, in an article entitled, "The Rapid Increase of the Tobacco Habit," says:—

"The amount spent in the United States alone for tobacco, annually, would enable me to provide thirty thousand families each year with all the necessities of life. In addition, I could grant an allowance of $5,000 to each of ten thousand other families. To each of ten thousand others I could give $10,000. To each of one thousand other heads of families, I could make a Christmas present of $50,000. To each of another thousand I could give $100,000; and, besides, to each of five hundred of my best friends I could make an annual allowance of $1,000,000. After doing all this, I would still have left each year, $200,000,000 to bestow on charitable institutions, and at least $10,000,-000 to keep the wolf from the door. Four hundred years ago the use of tobacco was unknown in civilized lands. To-day it is used by men, women, and children. Degeneracy has been the result. What the coming generations will be, if this craze continues to increase as it has in the past, does not present a picture pleasing to contemplate."
—*Temperance Instructor for 1911.*

In 1910, while traveling in Northern Michigan, I met Mr. A——, a business man of Grand Rapids. He said he had never used Tobacco. He had two boys who had never used the weed. He owns a nice home, his boys are strong and healthy; the older one is a prominent athlete at the Y. M. C. A. Mr. A—— said he was one day calling on a neighbor who asked why Mr. A—— was able to own a home, while he could not.

While they were talking, the elder son of Mr. G—— came in and said, "Give me a cigar, dad." The father replied, "They are all gone. Go to the store and buy a box." When the son returned, father and son each took a cigar. In a short time the younger son, a boy of sixteen or seventeen, came and asked for a cigar and was told, "There's the box, help yourself!"

They could not afford a home, but could afford to buy cigars by the box. In the twenty years of married life of that man, *he had burned up a home,* was setting a bad example for his boys, and allowing them to use a poison that was injuring them. Mr. G—— and his two sons were not up to the standard of Mr. A——and his sons, physically, mentally, financially. Why? — Tobacco. A word to the wise is sufficient. A noted man once said, "*Let your competitor smoke.*"

TOBACCO AND THE CIGARETTE

PART THREE—PHYSICAL EFFECT

Tobacco in any form is a deadly poison, deteriorating the bodily forces, deading to the finer sensibilities, and destructive to the finer mental and moral preceptions. But above every other evil, the effects of the Cigarette upon children and youth is the most deadly.

Testimony of Athletes and Athletic Directors

HE star batter of the Philadelphia Athletics, "Home Run Baker," says: "I don't drink nor smoke. Never did drink nor smoke. If any youngster wants advice from one who doesn't mean to preach, there it is. Leave cigarettes and tobacco in any form alone, and don't touch 'booze' now or at any time. It's the usual advice and doesn't carry much weight as a rule, but coming from a ball-player perhaps it may mean a little more to the American boy. Mine is the total-abstinence platform for both liquor and tobacco."

"The Cigarette is more harmful than whisky."—*Joseph H. Thompson, Coach of the Foot-Ball and Track Team of the University of Pittsburg.*

"I believe that the Cigarette is the one thing that is keeping many young men from developing the best that is in them, not only physically, but mentally and morally."—*E. E. Bliss, Physical Director, Oakland, Calif., Y. M. C. A.*

"A man's training is given to increase his endurance; so he must leave tobacco alone; for all trainers know that the use of it will effect the use of the heart's action."—*C. H. Price, Y. M. C. A. Physical Director, Los Angeles, Calif.*

"Whenever it is desired to secure the highest possible working ability by the organism, as in athletic contests, where the maximum of effort is demanded, all motor-depressant influences are removed as far as possible, *tobacco being one of the first substances forbidden.*"—*Jay W. Seaver, A. M., M. D., Medical Examiner of the Yale University Gymnasium.*

Tobacco Dwarfs

The average American boy wants to become an athlete. He should know that *tobacco will stunt the growth,*—a fact that is proved by medical men and educators who have given careful attention to the subject. Here are a few statements on this point:—

" There is nothing that so stunts the growth of boys and young men of the present day, as the use of tobacco."—*Physical Director Denver Y. M. C. A.*

" Personally, I have examined over fourteen thousand young men, and from general observation I can say that smoking has had its effect most particularly on the nervous system of the growing lad, as well as hindering his physical development."—*A. G. Studer, Acting General Secretary, Detroit Y. M. C. A.*

" We have carried on a series of observations relative to smokers. We find that smoking is *injurious* to *growing boys* and youth; that the smoker does not attain and hold as high a stand in the university as the non-smoker does. His *physical development* is *not so good,* and his *lung capacity* is usually lower than that of the non-smoker. I have no hesitation in saying that I consider the use of nicotin harmful for a growing youth."—*W. G. Anderson, M. A., M. D., Director of Yale University Gymnasium.*

" Unquestionably the most important matter in the health history of the students at this academy is that relating to the use of tobacco. I have urged upon the superintendent, as my last official utterance, the fact of the truth of which five years' experience as a health officer of the station has satisfied me, that beyond all other things, the future health and usefulness of the lads educated at this school, require the absolute interdiction of tobacco. In this opinion I have been sustained not only by all of my colleagues, but by all other sanitarians in civil and military life whose views I have been able to learn."—*Report of Dr. Albert L. Gihon, Senior Medical Officer of the Naval Academy at Annapolis, Md.*

"Tobacco is ruinous in our schools and colleges, dwarfing *body and mind.*"—*Dr. Willard Parker.*

" I shall not hesitate to pronounce tobacco in young men to be evil, and only evil, physically, mentally, and morally."—*Edward Hitchcock, of Amherst College.*

" In recent years there has been a decided increase in the number of sudden deaths from heart failure. There is no doubt that this increase is partially due to the free use of tobacco. *Nicotin strikes a direct blow at the heart.* It *weakens the heart's acion,* and in time brings about degenerative changes in its structure and also in the walls of the blood vessels. The hypertension and arteriosclerosis indicative of degenerative changes, are usually found among users of tobacco." — *Dr. Kress.*

TOBACCO AND THE CIGARETTE

PART FOUR — MORAL AND MENTAL EFFECTS

If *one sin* breaks through the door,
It will soon *make room* for more;
Shut the door against the first,
Then you'll never meet the worst.

C. M. Willis, Page 96, Temperance Torchlights.

"Out of six hundred in the State prison at Auburn, N. Y., sent there for crimes committed through strong drink, five hundred testified that it was *tobacco* that led them to *intemperance.*"—*Meta Lander.*

" Smoking and chewing tobacco, by rendering water and other simple liquids insipid to the taste, dispose very much to the use of ardent spirits. Hence the practice of smoking cigars has been followed by the use of brandy and water as a common drink."—*Dr. Benj. Rush, Formerly Professor of Chemistry and Theory and Practice of Medicine in Philadelphia Medical College.*

"The use of tobacco among the young is productive of mental and moral deterioration, while in the older persons, the use of the weed produces brain diseases and insanity. I have had a large experience in brain diseases, and am satisfied that smoking is the most noxious habit. I know of *no other cause or agent* that so much tends to bring on functional diseases, and through this, in the end, leads to *organic diseases of the brain.*"—*Dr. Solly, of St. Thomas Hospital, of England.*

" In all my twenty-five years' experience as a teacher, I have never known an exception to the rule, that a boy in taking on the tobacco habit in any form, immediately begins to deteriorate mentally. If he takes Cigarettes he will degenerate morally very rapidly, and physically, too. I am firmly convinced that tobacco in any form degenerates morally as it relates to growing boys."—*H. H. Cully, Principal Glenville High School, Cleveland, Ohio.*

" It is more difficult to restore an inebriate who persists in the use of tobacco. In some cases when tobacco is given up, all desire for spirits disappear."—*T. D. Crothers, M. D., Editor Journal of Inebriety.*

"So inseparable are the habits of drinking and smoking, that in some places the same word expresses both. Thus, the word 'peeud,' in the Bengalia language, signifies 'to drink' and 'to smoke.' "—Clarke.

" The inebriate who uses tobacco, has always a weaker nervous system than one who does not. Tobacco undoubtedly predisposes to, and encourages the use of, alcohol. In all cases it has an appreciable injurious effect upon the nerve-centers."—*T. D. Crothers, M. D., Editor Journal of Inebriety.*

(239)

A Nuisance,—The Smoker

"Signs may threaten, men may warn him,
  Babies cry, and women coax,
But he cares not one iota;
  For he calmly smokes and smokes."

TOBACCO AND THE CIGARETTE

PART FIVE—SPIRITUAL EFFECTS

" I beseech you therefore, brethren, by the mercies of God, that ye present your bodies a living sacrifice, holy, acceptable unto God, which is your reasonable service."

" If any man defile the temple of God, him shall God destroy; for the temple of God is holy, which temple ye are."—Paul.

Yet professed Christians, and even ministers of the gospel, will saturate themselves with the filthy weed tobacco in some of its forms, filling their blood with the nicotin poison until a leech placed upon the arm will fall dead inside of sixty seconds.

No one can so debase and deaden his physical system without impairing his mental powers. When the mental powers are thus degraded, and the faculties so impaired, just to that extent is the power to give God " reasonable service " destroyed.

Of course it is to professed Christian tobacco users that this chapter is presented. And to them we will say that their evil example is the argument behind which boy and men tobacco users hide, and by which they defend their use of the weed. Tens of thousands of boys are going to ruin physically, mentally, and morally because of the evil example of professed Christians, prominent educators, and physicians.

A Clean Ministry

"Be ye clean that bear the vessels of the Lord."—Isaiah.

A prominent church man once related the following experience ;—

" I used to use tobacco. When I gave it up I had a hard time for ten weeks. I was unable to sleep at night, would walk the floor, but God gave me victory."

Josiah Strong, in his "Challenge for the Churches" (page 267), does some interesting figuring. He says:—

" There are 20,000,000 Protestant church members in the United States. About one-third of them are males. Assuming that only one-half of the male membership are smokers (and we are afraid it is a very generous supposition), there are 3,333,000 in that class,

16

On the supposition that each smoke only three five-cent cigars a day, they together spend $500,000 daily for tobacco."

How the Deacon Took the Tobacco Cure

An evangelist conducting a revival service in Marietta, Ohio, relates the following incident : —

One of the deacons of the church, a very earnest man, was addicted to the use of tobacco. He was teacher of a large class of young ladies, and was very anxious that they should all be brought to Christ before the meeting closed. At the beginning of the series of services he brought me a list of the unconverted ones, and requested that I should pray and work for their conversion. We had a short talk concerning his class, and he seemed worried about his influence with them. As the week wore on and none of them were converted, he became more and more uneasy.

On Sunday morning he came to me with tears in his eyes and said he was going to make *a confession* to the class. I asked him what it was, and he replied: "I have been a slave to tobacco. I can not stand before these girls and plead with them to accept Christ with the taste of that vile stuff in my mouth. I promised God I would stop it last night. This morning when the appetite for it came on, the *devil* told me I couldn't. I am going to tell the girls about it this morning and ask them to pray for me."

When the Sunday-school hour was about half over I looked into his class room. All the heads were bowed in prayer, and most of the girls had their handkerchiefs to their faces, and were crying. As I closed the door softly I heard one of them praying, "Dear Jesus, *cure* our teacher."

You wouldn't have known that class of girls when they came out of the class room that day. Their indifference seemed to be all gone. The deacon followed them into the auditorium, and there he met his partner in the grocery store.

"John," he said, his face all aglow, "*I've taken the to-bacco cure.*"

"What is it?" asked his partner.

"I won't tell you now, John; but if it cures me will you take it too?"

"Sure," replied the partner.

"Shake hands on it," said the deacon.

They clasped hands, and in a few weeks afterward the deacon kept him to his word.

The deacon's tobacco cure was the inspiration of the meeting. Inside of three weeks *every girl in that class had accepted Christ,* and they didn't stop at that, either. Many others were brought to Christ through their efforts. And so the deacon's tobacco cure became "the cure of souls."—*Stephen J. Corey, in the Christian Endeavor World.*

An Appeal to Christians.

But what can be done to teach children and youth the evils of a practice of which *parents, teachers, and ministers* set them the *example?* Little boys hardly emerged from babyhood may be seen smoking their Cigarettes. If one speaks to them about it they say, "My father uses tobacco." They *point to the minister* or the *Sunday-school superintendent,* and say, "Such a man smokes; what harm for me to do as he does?" *Many workers in the temperance cause use tobacco.* What power can such persons have to stay the progress of intemperance?

I appeal to those who profess to believe and obey the Word of God: Can you as a Christian indulge in a habit that is paralyzing your intellect, and robbing you of power rightly to estimate eternal realities? Can you consent daily to *rob God of service* which is his due, and *to rob your fellow men,* both of service you might render, and of the power of example?

Have you considered your responsibilities as God's stewards for the means in your hands? How much of the Lord's money do you spend for tobacco? Reckon up what you have thus spent during your lifetime. How does the amount consumed by this defiling lust compare with what you have given for the relief of the poor and the spread of the gospel?

No human being needs tobacco, but *multitudes* are *perishing* for want of the means that by its use is worse than wasted.—*Ministry of Healing.*

TOBACCO AND THE CIGARETTE

PART SIX—THE CIGARETTE

THE question is often asked, "Why is the Cigarette doing more harm than the other forms of Tobacco?" We answer : —

First, because the user of the Cigarette is *more apt to inhale* than the user of pipe or cigars.

"When tobacco smoke is inhaled [breated into the lungs], the nicotin enters the cerebral circulation directly and benumbs the brain. It enters the larynx and bronchial tubes, coating their membrane with carbon and acting as an irritant."

Second, because the combination of the tobacco and the paper in the Cigarette form several poisons that are injurious. They are:—

Prussic Acid: the most deadly poison known.

Acrolein: rated in any standard book of chemistry as second only to prussic acid in its deadly effect. In Webster's International Dictionary, 1901, it is defined as "A limpid, colorless, highly volatile liquid. Its vapors are intensely irritating."

Pyridine: "It is the nucleus of a large number of organic substances, among which several alkaloids, as nicotin, ... may be mentioned."

Carbonic Oxide or Monoxide gas: "Carbonic oxide (chem.) : a colorless gas. C. O. of slight odor, called more correctly *Carbon Monoxide.* It is the product of the incomplete combustion of carbon. . . . It is fatal to animal life."

Besides these poisons, nicotin is always present in tobacco in any form,— giving a total of *five poisons in the Cigarette.*

Third, Ignorance of the effects of Cigarettes on the human being. The Cigarette being so small, and the white paper so clean in appearance, thousands of innocent people are entrapped and ruined physically, mentally, and morally, by those *"Little White Devils."* It has been estimated that from *one thousand two hundred to one thousand five hundred boys begin smoking every day.*

Women and Baby Smokers

In 1909, I was invited to speak at a woman's missionary meeting, at Washington, D. C. At the close of the meeting an elderly lady asked for literature giving statements as to the effect of Cigarettes. She said she had a married daughter that was smoking Cigarettes, and *teaching her little three-year-old boy to smoke!*

I knew a woman who began smoking Cigarettes. I was shocked when I heard that she had placed a Cigarette in the mouth of her sweet little four-year-old girl. I tell you that made me mad! I said then that I would do all I could to knock out Cigarettes. A young married lady told me that her husband was a "Cigarette fiend." He was dopy most of the time. When not under the influence of Cigarettes, he was restless, nervous, irritable, and unkind. Life to her became a burden.

"A Cigarette dealer in Philadelphia states that he sells one hundred fifty thousand Cigarettes a month to women who come in carriages, and send footmen to buy."

A World Wide Evil

Dr. Clinton says that "a good deal has been said about the evils of Cigarette smoking; but not one half the truth has ever been told."

Not only in America, but in every land, in every clime, is the effect of the Cigarette seen. In *China,* where such a successful crusade against opium was made, the tobacco people from our own civilized America went with an un-limited amount of advertising matter, and sample packages of Cigarettes, which were scattered broadcast, and now the Cigarette habit threatens to be a *greater curse than opium was!*

Effects Upon School Boys

A physician's statement:—

"*Cigarette smoking first blunts the whole* moral nature. It has an appalling effect upon the physical system as well. It *first stimulates, then stupefies the nerves. It sends boys into consumption.* It gives *them enlargement of the heart* and it *sends them to the insane asylum!*

"I am often called in to prescribe for boys for palpitation of the heart. In nine cases out of ten this is caused by the Cigarette habit. I have seen *bright boys turned into dunces,* and *straightforward, honest boys made miserable cowards* by Cigarette smoking. I am speaking the truth,—nearly every physician and every teacher knows." —*Dr. A. Clinton.*

In a school of 500 pupils, a careful investigation ex-tending over several months was made, and briefly summed up, shows the following:—

"The average efficiency of the *non-smokers* in that school was ninety-five per cent, in other words, ninety-five out of every one hundred were reasonably sure of getting at least a good common school education, while of the *Cigarette fiends*, only five to ten per cent stand any show in school, and they are *two and one-fifth years behind in their own grade*, and more than *three years behind the girls they started with in the first grade*.

" The teachers who made this investigation expressed themselves to the parents of the boys as follows:—

" We desire to call attention to the fact that a *large majority* of the boys of this city are smoking Cigarettes; that the boys who are smoking are, on an average, years behind the boys who do not smoke; and still farther behind the girls in the same grades; that the *mental, moral*, and *physical condition* of many of these boys is *extremely deplorable*, and will certainly continue to grow worse unless the habit is stopped; that while the schools are insisting that this and other unclean and undesirable habits shall not be practiced in or about the school house or grounds; still, crowds of our boys are daily seen around the saloons and loafing places of our streets, smoking, *loafing, swearing*, and *cultivating other undesirable habits*.

" This was *plain talk*, and it had *immediate* effect. It is estimated that seventy-five per cent of the Cigarette smoking by boys was stopped. What was called the worst school in the country, is now spoken of as doing good work. *The school board raised the salary of the teachers and principal* twenty-five per cent. The people are pleased. The improved condition of the boys is noticeable in their *language, dress, manners, efficiency*, and especially in their *moral tone*.

"The former principal and superintendent smoked."

But think! that is but one school among thousands in America that is wasting money in trying to *educate numb- skulls!* Bob Burdette, in his comical way, says:—

" *My son, as long as thou hast in thy skull the sense of a jay bird, break away from the Cigarette, for lo, it causeth thy breath to stink like a glue factory; it rendereth thy mind less intelligent than that of a cigar store dummy, yea, thou art a cipher with the rim knocked off.*"

When you rub the rim off a cipher you have less than nothing.

Theodore Roosevelt expresses himself as follows : —

" If you are going to do anything permanent for the average man, you have got to begin before he is a man. The chance of success lies in working with the boy, and not with the man."—*Theodore Roosevelt*.

Bad Example of Educators and School Men

Superintendent J. K. McBroom, in an address to educators, said in part:—

" What will we do with a superintendent who uses tobacco? Send him to the legislature? Legislative atmosphere seems to be *mostly to-*

bacco smoke anyway. Send him to the reform school, I was going to say; then I remembered that wouldn't do, for that of course is only for youthful offenders for whom there yet lingers hope of reformation."

Speaking of boys, Mr. McBroom says:—

" Now is the time of most urgent need that every safeguard and every vigilant precaution be thrown around them to save them from the vile habits and tendencies which they are exposed on every hand, and which if allowed to get their grip now, will handicap the boys all their lives, and in many cases ruin them for any further effective or ambitious effort.

" Chief among these vices, because usually the *first* to gain a foothold, is the use of tobacco; and that seems to be the *father* of all the rest. It *breeds deception* at the very start, *in every single case,* I believe; bad company, and even worse meeting places; *dwarfed ambition, sluggish intellect.*

" Now if the young man has any *capacity or inclination* in the line of school work, we have the strongest possible appeal to his *pride and his ambition* in telling him that the use of tobacco is absolutely ruinous to good scholarship. But the pupil will find a *fatal flaw* in the logic if the superintendent himself uses tobacco; for almost inevitably in the mind of the pupil, the superintendent is a *notable example of high scholarship.* The best teaching, except for some rudiments and routine of instruction is mostly a matter of intangible atmosphere; the *right kind of influence,* contact and association of the pupil with a *strong, clean, wholesome personality* in the teacher. Now if superintendent or college professor or any other schoolman, has one *conspicuous weakness; one habit* that is universally considered a bad habit, he fails in exactly the most important point; and though he may be strong as an *instructor, disciplinarian, administrator,* yet he will be weak as an *educator, as a maker of character.*

"He may surround himself with a corps of strong, loyal young men and women, who will attend to the education of the pupils, while he attends to the administration of the system; but even then, his own influence in the development of character in the pupils will be zero or a negative quantity. Now that kind of influence might answer in the management of *a railroad* or *a packing house,* but in the administration of a school it is *not good enough.*

What can we say to the boys when they quote the example of physicians, college professors, school superintendents, ministers of the gospel, churchmen, and even their own fathers? Such men should read the following statement with care : —

"There is something about this Cigarette habit that weakens and unnerves the boy. It *destroys his memory,* impairs his other cognitive faculties, robs him of his power of attention, saps his will-power, and deprives him of his initiative; he *becomes tremulous and timid,* and fears to do the things he would.

"Often this filthy and disgusting habit has so fastened itself upon the impressionable boy nature, that it can not be shaken off. *What base slavery!* What bonds of vice that *eat like canker* into the physical being of its victim!

"Many physicians with whom I consulted in the matter have assured me of the effect of tobacco upon the growing boy, and all have regarded the Cigarettes as the most pernicious form of tobacco using. Do *college professors,* and *college men,* and other users of Cigarettes who are in a position to influence boys, ever think of their *responsibility* for the bad example they give? How can advice to refrain from the Cigarette be heeded when it comes from one who is himself a user of the Cigarette?"—*Wm. H. DeLacy, Judge of the Juvenile Court, Washington, D. C.*

Boy Criminals and the Cigarette

Judge Ben. B. Lindsey, of Denver, known as "The Boys' Judge, says:—

"The Cigarette not only has a *grip upon boyhood,* but it invites *all other* demons of habit to come and add to the *degradation.*"

Another writer says : —

"There is no surer way for the young boy to procure as associates the criminal and immoral, than for him to begin the smoking of Cigarettes; the use of the Cigarette draws to him the older and more vicious who are ready to initiate him into that kind of life which paves his way to destruction."

In testimony of the grip which the Cigarette habit obtains upon boys, and its tendency to crime, read carefully the following statement from Abraham Bowers, Immigration Secretary of the Y. M. C. A. of Chicago : —

"It gives me pleasure to endorse the work of the Anti-Cigarette League. While I was teacher of the boys in the Cook County jail. I found that almost every one of them could attribute his downfall partly to the use of Cigarettes. They were the *most seriously afflicted* with the habit of any class of boys I have ever known. They desired to have a recess every forty-five minutes to go outside the room to smoke a Cigarette. At night frequently about two or three o'clock in the morning, some of them would be *aroused from their sleep* for the want of a Cigarette, and not having it they would *pound the cells,* and wake all the other boys and men in the jail, if necessary to get the Cigarettes. Many of them admitted that they had *been led to steal* originally to get money with which to buy Cigarettes."

The following statement is from the pen of Judge Leroy B. Crane, of New York : —

"Cigarettes are ruining our children, *endangering their lives,* dwarfing their intellects, and making them *criminals* fast. The boys who use them seem to lose all sense of *right, decency, and righteousness.* To have great men requires the most forceful means to check this pernicious and death-dealing habit. Ask the mothers of the land to help you and they will respond.

"In my court *ninety-five per cent* of the boys brought before me charged with offenses from *shooting crap* to *burglary* are Cigarette smokers, while those who do not smoke them seldom appear before me.

"This morning three boys were brought before me for petty larceny, the oldest eighteen, the youngest sixteen,—the stain of Cigarettes on their fingers, and the mothers there to accompany their boys. I was compelled to send one to the reform school at the mother's request; the other two were placed on probation to give them another start.

"I call Cigarettes Little White Devils. The U. S. government should pass laws preventing their sale and manufacture within its borders."

Of the tendency of the Cigarette to promote crime and insanity, the following experience will testify : —

"Of all the juvenile criminals tried in my court, not *one for years* has been found free from the *stain of Cigarettes* on his thumb and first two fingers. Of all the *lunatics* tried in my court, an attempt is made to learn the cause of lunacy, and in *more than half* Cigarette smoking is assigned as the cause."—*Judge Baker, Louisville, Ky.*

"It does seem, as one stated, 'that either the smoking of Cigarettes *causes insanity, or that it is the insane who smoke.*'"

Says Thomas A. Edison : —

"Acrolein is one of the *most terrible drugs* in its effect on the human body. The *burning of* ordinary *cigarette paper always produces acrolein.* That is what makes the smoke so irritating. I really believe that it often *makes boys insane.* We sometimes develop acrolein in this laboratory in our experiments with glycerine. One whiff of it from the oven drove one of my assistants out of the building the other day. I *can hardly exaggerate the dangerous nature of acrolein,* and yet that is what a man or a boy is dealing with every time he smokes an ordinary Cigarette."

"*The blood of persons poisoned by the inhalation of illuminating gas,* rich in carbonic oxide, is found to be *coagulated* and *indurated,* and may be pulled in strings from the *veins and arteries.*

"Owing to the loose structure of the Cigarette, its combustion is modified and destructive distillation proceeds with combustion, and owing to the incompleteness of oxidation, carbonic oxide is largely produced instead of carbonic acid. This carbonic oxide inhaled into the lungs enters the blood unresisted, and the damage it does is in direct proportion to the quantities inhaled. *Carbonic oxide when inhaled in small quantities produces faintness, dizziness, palpitation of the heart, and a feeling of great heaviness in the feet and legs.* These are exactly the effects of the Cigarette and *the depression* and *nervousness* which follow as a reaction make the *victim crave* some *balm or tonic* for his malaise. He is then led to consume the drug in ever increasing quantities."

Notice the following prison record : —

"On the first day of this month we had 278 boys between the ages of ten and fifteen. Ninety-two per cent of the whole number were in the habit of smoking Cigarettes at the time they committed the crimes for which they were sent to the reformatory. Eighty-five per cent had become so addicted to their use as to be classed at the time as 'Cigarette fiends.' Of 4,117 boys received into the reformatory since its organization on June 8, 1893, ninety-five per cent were in the habit of using tobacco, and nearly all were Cigarette smokers. Consequently we see that the Cigarette is a great factor in developing criminals."—*Hon Geo. Torrence, formerly Superintendent of Illinois State Reformatory.*

Reliable testimony : —

"I regard the Cigarette as a *fuse of infernal* fire, tending to explode the *worst passions of the body!* In dealing with more than sixteen thousand delinquent children during the last eight years, I find as a rule the user of Cigarettes is a *stunt, a weakling in body, mind, and morals.*"—*Zed H. Copp, Chief Probation Officer, Juvenile Court, Washington, D. C.*

Heart Tracings

We invite your attention to the work of the delicate little instrument, called the sphygmograph, which records the strength and regularity of the heart beat. Notice the following tracings:—

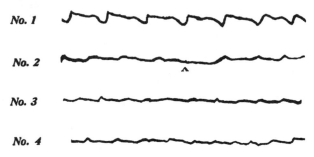

No. 1 shows a healthy heart beat. No. 2, the heart beat of a young man while smoking. Where the mark ᴧ is, you will notice that the heart skipped a full beat. No. 3, after smoking, with a partial skip in the heart beat, even while under the stimulus of tobacco. No. 4, the heart beat of a tobacco user.

The tobacco heart has become a prominent feature in the medical diagnosis of the day.

Danger to Growing Boys

This progressive use of the Cigarette is especially true with boys in the period of rapid growth. The wreath of Cigarette smoke which curls about the head of the growing lad *holds his brain in an iron grip* which prevents it from growing and his mind from developing just as surely as the iron shoe does the foot of the Chinese girl.

In the terrible struggle for survival against the deadly Cigarette smoke, development and growth are sacrificed by nature, which in the fight for very life itself, must yield up every vital luxury such as healthy body growth and growth of brain and mind.

If all boys could be made to know that with every breath of Cigarette smoke they *inhale imbecility* and *exhale manhood;* that they are tapping their arteries as surely and letting their life blood out as truly as though their *veins and arteries were severed,* and that the Cigarette is a maker of *invalids, criminals,* and *fools*—not men— it ought to deter them some. *The yellow finger stains is an emblem of deeper degredation and enslavement than the ball and chain.*

Hudson Maxim.

Cigarette School Boy   A Few Years Later

Business Men and the Cigarette

How do employers of men and boys rate the Cigarette smoker? Read the following terse statements : —

"We might as well go to the *insane asylum* for our men as to employ Cigarette smokers."—*The late E. H. Harriman, Railroad King.*

"Never advance the pay of a Cigarette smoker; never *promote him*; never *trust him.*"—*Elbert Hubbard.*

"More and more young men are hoisting the sign, 'I am a fool,' by appearing in public with a Cigarette."—*P. M. Sharpless, Cream Separator Maunfacturer.*

"The use of intoxicating liquor by men, and the use of Cigarettes by boys, is creating a race of *feeble-minded, unhealthy,* and *valueless citizens.*"—*John Wanamaker.*

"We do not employ boys in the Larkin office, who smoke Cigarettes. An applicant addicted to the use of Cigarettes would hardly interest us; but if he seemed to possess qualifications that made him desirable, he would have to *decide between Cigarettes and the job.*"—*Wm. R. Heath, Vice-President Larkin Company, Buffalo.*

The notice which follows was posted throughout the factory of the Cadillac Motor Company, Nov. 28, 1911:

"Cigarette smoking is acquiring a hold on a great many boys in our community; the habit has grown to an abnormal extent among boys and men in the last year or two. Since it is such a bad practice, and is taking such a hold upon so many people, we think it a *disgrace* for a grown man to smoke a Cigarette, because it is not only injurious to his health, but is such a *bad example* to the boys.

"Boys who smoke Cigarettes, we do *not care to employ* or to *keep in our employ.* In the future *we will not hire any one* whom we know to be addicted to this habit. It is our desire to weed it entirely out of our factory just as soon as practicable. We will ask every one in our factory who sees the seriousness of this habit to use his influence in having it stamped out. We have two objects in interesting ourselves in this matter. First, to help men and boys; second, *We believe that men who do not smoke Cigarettes or frequent saloons, can make better automobiles than those who do.*"

The following is an extract from the Fidelity, one of the oldest insurance companies in America:—

"After a careful investigation we have decided that we will not bond a man who uses Cigarettes, for such men *are not safe, physically or morally.*"

"I verily believe that the *mental force, power of labor,* and *endurance* of our profession is decreased at least twenty-five per cent by the use of tobacco."—*Ex-Senator Doolittle, in an address delivered to the graduating law class of Wisconsin University.*

Cigarettes and Tuberculosis

The claim made by Surgeon General Rixey of the United States navy that the smoking of Cigarettes is responsible for many of the cases of *pulmonary tuberculosis* that occur among the men of that body is an interesting one. *The Cigarette* has long been considered a *dangerous luxury,* and taking into consideration the opinion of Dr. Rixey, the statement that during the past three months the crew of the ship Missouri—700 men—used *one thousand five hundred books of Cigarette papers, one thousand two hundred pounds of tobacco* and *thirty-seven thousand Cigarettes*, the fact that the ratio of men suffering from *pulmonary troubles* in *our navy is larger than in the navies of either Germany or England*, is not surprising. As a matter of precaution and common sense, this devotion to the Cigarette should at least be curbed to a very great extent.—*Washington Post.*

"It has been brought to the attention of the bureau from many sources," says the surgeon general, "that Cigarette smoking is becoming a *serious impediment to robust health in the navy.* This habit seems to have taken a decided impetus in the service since the Spanish war and has spread to incredible proportions."—*The Deadly Cigarette, Lucy Page Gaston.*

Leads to Drinking and Opium

Dr. Chas. L. Hamilton, of the Keeley Institute, says: "The continual *dryness* of the mucous membranes of the mouth and pharynx, due to the *paralyzing influence* of the Cigarette on the nerve terminals and which the drinking of water will not relieve, is readily quenched by *alcoholic drinks*, and this discovery, once made by the Cigarette habitue, leads to frequent indulgence in liquor, and aided by the effort to combat malnutrition and its attendant weaknesses, almost invariably causes him to become an *alcoholic inebriate.*"

Also a quotation from Dr. B. Broughton, in charge of the opium department of the Keeley institute, Dwight, Ill.: "*More young men are led into the opium habit by Cigarette smoking* than by patent and proprietary medicines. *Sixty per cent of all males* under forty years of age, treated at Dwight for morphin, opium, or cocaine using in 1896 had been smokers of Cigarettes, and sixty per cent of these had no other excuse than that they needed some *stimulant* more than the Cigarette furnished them."

"Our experience here at Dwight, where many hundreds of Cigarette cases have been treated, is that persons applying for treatment for both liquor and cigarettes dread giving up their Cigarette more than they do the liquor. Moreover, those who return to the use of Cigarettes in after-life, are almost certain to resume the use of liquor to allay the irritability of the nervous system produced by tobacco smoke inhalation."—*Some Effects of Tobacco Using.*

Cigars and Fires

"Cigarettes for boys spell tragedy everywhere! The fire at Bangor last Sunday began with a careless smoker. The Baltimore fire, the Chelsea-Boston fire, the fire of the Windsor Hotel, New York, the Albany Statehouse fire, and the Horrible Triangle Waist Company holocaust, all of these, with charred human bodies, and wrecked homes and lives, are traced to the carelessness and brutal disregard accompanying the Cigarette habit.

"Fire Commissioner Waldo attributes 700 fires per year in New York to this cause. The *tobacco campanies* deny the evil of their product, and invite inspection of their premises and processes. But a mere inspection of the Cigarette boys, in the public schools and factories ought to be enough!"—*Editorial in Religious Weekly.*

Dangers of Inhaling

The following paragraphs are selected from "Confessions of a Cigarette Smoker in England."

"Inhaling consists simply in drawing a *volume of smoke* from the Cigarette into the mouth, and then taking a deep breath, in the act of which the smoke is carried from the mouth down into the lungs. . . .

"Let the nicotin fumes go where they may, in their passage they come into contact with the *nervous system*, and the result is an *instantaneous communication to the brain*, which takes the form of a momentary *semi-paralysis*—that is, when a man is new at the habit.

"I remember very well the experience of a youngster of *eighteen* on his being *taught to inhale* the smoke of a Cigarette for the first time. One afternoon some *friends persuaded* him to make the attempt, and he did so. Almost upon the instant he fell full length upon the floor in a *dead faint;* and his features became pallid, his *pulse faint and irregular;* and those about him were for a time in a great fright. A day or two later he tried to inhale again, with a result *not quite* so bad; and he went on trying till now he is a *veritable slave* to the habit.

"A leading tobacconist in the city of London told me that in the space of five years he had seen *regular frequenters* of his shop completely *broken down in mind and body* through having contracted the inhaling habit; moreover, that some of them were in the cemetery who, he was convinced, need not have been there. Of course, the medical certificate did not give inhaling tobacco smoke as the cause. Very likely it said consumption. But I can quite believe, and so can any confirmed inhaler, that it was the Cigarette that was the cause of it all.

"The moral of all this is a simple one. *Never upon any consideration* be tempted to inhale for the first time. Probably this *initial attempt* would lead to the establishment of the habit, with all the sad consequences I have enumerated. And, as I indicated at the outset, breaking away from it is such a difficult matter that *not one person in a thousand* ever succeeds in the attempt. Inhaling is one of those habits which *can not be broken off by degrees.* The division must be drawn *sharp and clean*, and there must be no smoking of any sort. To the confirmed inhaler this system of cure is a painful one; but it is the only one I have known to succeed."

A Sure Cure

"I have found a way to cure Jimmy of smoking Cigarettes," said Mrs. Maloney over the back fence to Mrs. O'Brien.

"And what is that?"

"By the laying on of hands. It is a great remedy and a sure cure."